"Jennifer O'Toole's new book *The Asperkid's Game Plan* is loaded with fun and educational activities that will keep your child engaged at home, in the car, and on those long, boring vacation drives. Jennifer outlines different learning styles so that the reader can assess their own child to find the right activities that will help with such things as attention, reciprocity, sensory issues, auditory processing and identifying emotions. In each chapter she targets a specific psycho-social skill with a fun activity using every day materials from your own home. *The Asperkid's Game Plan* is a well-thought out book that presents an alternative to tedious exercises. Suggestions for academic and educational reinforcement are included. The beautiful colors and layout of the book presents a delightful, instructive book that will benefit any child."

—*Debra Houssini, parent and founder of The Art of Autism*

"Jennifer O'Toole wins again with *The Asperkid's Game Plan*, and so do we—the teachers, parents, and clinicians who are looking for ways to be better communicators and educators for our Asperkids. Every child wants to learn, especially those on the autism spectrum, and it's up to us to reach and teach them using methods that will foster their unique abilities and learning strengths. O'Toole's 'Game Plan' is insightful, empowering, and packed full of purposeful play activities that are easy to do and mind-blowingly fun!"

—*Jodi Murphy, founder of Geek Club Books and mother of an Asperkid*

"With the precision of a scientist combined with the artistry of an experienced educator, Jennifer O'Toole has crafted a game changer of a curriculum in the holistic education of children (of all ages!) on the autism spectrum. 'Standard' school subjects are seamlessly integrated with developing greater understanding of the self and the universe surrounding us all. This resource is invaluable to anyone wanting direct instruction in successfully educating those with autism—and everyone else as well."

—*Stephen M. Shore, Ed.D., Assistant Professor of Special Education at Adelphi University, author, consultant and presenter on issues related to autism*

"Jennifer O'Toole has created a colorful and brilliant work of genius. Therapists of all disciplines will cherish this book. It is a must-buy for every clinic! Jennifer has broken down each awesome activity into its component skills so you don't have to when treatment planning! It is guaranteed to spark creativity while teaching skills for success! What could be better than pairing fun activities with learning? A definite must-read."

—*Cara Koscinski, occupational therapist, author of* The Pocket Occupational Therapist for Families of Children with Special Needs *and mother to two children with autism*

by the same author

The Asperkid's (Secret) Book of Social Rules
The Handbook of Not-So-Obvious
Social Guidelines for Tweens and
Teens with Asperger Syndrome
Jennifer Cook O'Toole
Illustrated by Brian Bojanowski
ISBN 978 1 84905 915 2
eISBN 978 0 85700 685 1

Asperkids
An Insider's Guide to Loving, Understanding and
Teaching Children with Asperger Syndrome
Jennifer Cook O'Toole
Foreword by Liane Holliday Willey
ISBN 978 1 84905 902 2
eISBN 978 0 85700 647 9

The Asperkid's Launch Pad
Home Design to Empower
Everyday Superheroes
Jennifer Cook O'Toole
ISBN 978 1 84905 931 2
eISBN 978 0 85700 727 8

The Asperkid's Not-Your-Average-Coloring-Book
Jennifer Cook O'Toole
ISBN 978 1 84905 958 9

EXTRAORDINARY MINDS,
PURPOSEFUL PLAY...ORDINARY STUFF

THE ASPERKID'S
GAME PLAN

JENNIFER COOK O'TOOLE

Jessica Kingsley *Publishers*
London and Philadelphia

Illustrations on pages 23 and 81 reproduced from Cook O'Toole
2012 with kind permission from Brian Bojanowski.
Photograph on page 82 reproduced with kind permission
from Beanforest (www.beanforest.etsy.com).

First published in 2014
by Jessica Kingsley Publishers
73 Collier Street
London N1 9BE, UK
and
400 Market Street, Suite 400
Philadelphia, PA 19106, USA

www.jkp.com

Copyright © Jennifer Cook O'Toole 2014
Photographs copyright © Kristen Giuliano and Jennifer Cook O'Toole 2014

Front cover images source: Kristen Giuliano

Library of Congress Cataloging in Publication Data
A CIP catalog record for this book is available from the Library of Congress

British Library Cataloguing in Publication Data
A CIP catalogue record for this book is available from the British Library

ISBN 978 1 84905 959 6
eISBN 978 0 85700 779 7

Printed and bound in China

FOR LORI, BECAUSE YOU WILL
ALWAYS MAKE ME SMILE.

TRUE FRIENDSHIP ISN'T ABOUT
BEING INSEPARABLE.

IT'S BEING SEPARATED...AND
NOTHING CHANGES.

ACKNOWLEDGMENTS

The biggest thank you goes to my own kids, who ignored the cameras in their faces and, even when they had already done the very crafts, activities and games featured in this book, helped recreate what Mom had badly photographed or managed to delete from iPhoto.

Thank you, Maura, Sean and Gavin, for knowing that I'd play every game with you a hundred times over even if no one else noticed or cared.

To Kristen Giuliano, photographer, thank you for helping to make the fun possible.

Thanks to Toni Schulken, MS, OTR/L, Founder of Pathways for Learning, for identifying and bullet pointing the skill sets being practiced by the *Game Plan*.

Thanks to my mom, as always, for the practicalities—pick-ups and grocery trips and everything in-between that gave me the time for all the craziness herein.

And always the Grand Finale, to John, my husband and teammate. May we, too, remember to take the time to laugh and play as we travel this crazy road together. I love you, John, and always, always will.

CONTENTS

Introduction 13

Chapter 1 Colored Rice, Three Dimensions and See-Through Eggshells:
The Foundational Role of Sensory Work. 32
Anxiety management, logical (non-reactive) thinking,
effective communication and flexible problem-solving.
Included Activities:
1. That's My Name, Don't Wear It Out 37
2. Blindfolded Geometry and Communication Lessons 42
3. Expandable Hearts and See-Through Eggshells. 52
Snapshot-Sized Fun: Sort It Out! 59
Snapshot-Sized Fun: Sensory Play to Go 62
Snapshot-Sized Fun: Lost and Found 64

Chapter 2 Human Knots and Cake: What it Means to Be Part of a Team. 66
Teamwork, collaboration and negotiation of roles.
Included Activities:
1. The Tray of Randomness 70
2. The Human Knot 74
3. Lego My Creation!. 77
4. Gaming: Extra Tips for Everyone. 81
Snapshot-Sized Fun: Where Do I Fit In? 84

Chapter 3 How Much "Matter" Can You Stuff in There?
Personal Priorities, Meet Your Team 86
Perspective-taking and impulsivity.
Included Activities:
1. Enter Mountain Pose 90
2. The Tower of Density 93

Chapter 4 The Forest, the Trees and the Sum of the Parts 100
Part-to-whole relationships, inclusion and perception versus fact.
Included Activities:
1. Bug's Eye View 105
2. Find That Analogy! 109
3. The "Pointillism" of Art 116
4. Supersize It! 121
Snapshot-Sized Fun: Glowing Water 124

Chapter 5 Illusions, Spy Games and Triangles: The (Continued)
Possibility of More than One Truth 126
Cognitive flexibility, listening skills and theory of mind.
Included Activities:
1. Gotcha! 132
2. Vanishing Points 136
3. Drawing Hands 139
4. Spy Games 141
5. Plastic Ice Cream Trucks 146
6. Constructive Triangles 150
7. Cast a (Paper) Net 157
Snapshot-Sized Fun: Cosmic Cleanup 165

Chapter 6 Paint Chip Emotions: Helping Your Asperkid "See" a Rainbow of Feelings 166
Absolutism, emotional awareness and emotional vocabulary.
Included Activities:
1. Color Math 173
2. Clip the Colors Fantastic. 177
3. Ombré Trend-ay 183
4. Socks and Charades 189
5. Planks in the Living Room 195
6. Not All Ick is Created Equal: Homemade Scratch-off Cards 198
Snapshot-Sized Fun: Contained Color Chaos 206

Chapter 7 Cracking, Poking and Popping: Breaking Through Rigidity and Letting Wonder In 208
Resistance to change, reciprocity and flexible thinking.
Included Activities:
1. Fried Marbles 211
2. Good Clean Fun: Petri Dishes, Geodes and Popsicles 215
3. Permissible Breakthroughs: Nine Ways to Play with Bubble Wrap 220
4. Pomanders, Tattooed Bananas and Constellations 224
Snapshot-Sized Fun: Slime. 'Nuff Said. 231

CONCLUSION. 233
APPENDIX 1: TRIANGLE CHALLENGES 235
APPENDIX 2: CAST-A-NET PAPER SHAPE TEMPLATES 238
RESOURCES FOR MORE FUN (AND UNDERCOVER DISCOVERIES) 243
REFERENCES 247

"LET THEM EAT CAKE."

REALLY. WITH FROSTING.

LIFE'S TOO SHORT TO
SKIMP ON THE FUN.

INTRODUCTION

Aloe Plants, Quarks and Misunderstandings: Fun That Matters

Perfect. You're just in time for a lecture on the various grasses growing in sixteenth-century Lithuania!

Wait. No! Don't shut the book! We could try something else! How about quark, hadrons and the debatable stability of fundamental constituents of matter?

No good, either? OK, last try. What if we go with:

All the Things You Do Badly: How and Why You Should Change Them or No One Will Ever Like You

Not so much, huh? Don't worry. I'm only kidding. The "grasses" thing might actually be boring enough to be considered torture by some international standard. I had to make the physics title up out of a Wikipedia entry. And I'm fairly certain that no one would be waiting at the ticket booth for Lecture 3.

In this way, and in many others, you are just like an Asperkid. No one likes being bored, no one likes feeling confused and no one likes to hear a litany of personal shortcomings. That's true for you. It's true for me. It's true for Asperkids, too. Yet for some reason, when adults set out to "help" young people on the spectrum, they completely lose perspective of what it would be like to be on the receiving end of said "help." Well-meaning therapists routinely drum up tedious activities, under-educated teachers misunderstand student challenges and parents endlessly criticize the very young people we all want to empower. Enter diagnosis, and exit common sense.

Now, let me be fair. I *know* it's tough parenting kids who demand constant vigilance, creativity and energy. I know because I have three Asperkids of my own. I *know* it's challenging to teach a class full of students, each of whom has individual needs to be met, while the adults try to navigate blurry lines between instructor, disciplinarian and traffic cop. I know because I, too, taught classes with too many pupils for the number of desks. I *know* it's hard to advise overstressed parents and counsel kids who don't want to hear one word you have to say. I know because I was a social worker and still coach families and Asperkids. Last, I *know* it's confusing, scary and lonely to be the kid with amazing brains who can't seem to figure out the basic rules everyone else plays by. To never know when or why the next rug will be pulled from under your feet. To be told, "Just go play like all the other kids," and have no clue at all how to begin. I know because I have Asperger Syndrome. And I've seen childhood on the spectrum through my own eyes.

Starting Off on the Wrong Foot: "Ass"umptions and Playgrounds

There is an old adage about making "ass"umptions. To take for granted that we know all there is to know about any situation is, truth be told, rather foolish… not to mention more than a bit arrogant.

Of course, all of us operate on some basic assumptions. I assume the sun will come up tomorrow, and expect to be right. But people are less predictable. If you yell at a child near the road, he may assume you are angry with him. The reality, though, is that you are frightened. Angry and scared look a lot alike. So do shy and stuck-up and overwhelmed and impatient. There's lots of room for mistakes when we assume that we know what is going on in someone else's mind or heart.

The most frequently incorrect assumption neurotypicals (NTs) make is that they *know* what Asperkids "look like." "But you're so normal," people will say to me, "and your kids are so smart!" Were you expecting aliens with three heads?

The truth is that "normal" is a setting on the dryer, and I don't know anyone who ever chose a hero because she was so "typical."

Heroes aren't "normal." They're extraordinary. (That's the point.)

www.Asperkids.com

Asperger Syndrome/autism is merely a different neurological hardwiring. It's not new, it's not wrong, it's not better and it's not worse. It's just different. I have red hair, and have since the moment I was born. I can't be "cured" of my gingerness any more than I can (or ought) to be "cured" of my Asperger's.

Like me, my sons, my daughter and my husband…like Emily Dickinson, Albert Einstein, Henry Ford and Marie Curie…we Aspies live alongside you, but we process and perceive the world very differently than you. It's the same life, but with the "volume" —of sound, light, touch, emotional intensity, thought, insecurity, sense of morality, justice and general creativity—turned way up. The same truths, but just spoken in "neurological dialects."

This autumn, our family visited England. And these kiddos were trying their darndest to "blend"—saying "Oi!" instead of "Hey!" (as they had learned from *Doctor Who*)… *heck,* my daughter even found a double-decker bus advertising one of her special interests!

But let's face it—natives we were not. Although he had been warned about differences in American versus British English, our six-year-old son did manage one spectacular gaff. As we crossed near an enormous puddle outside of Victoria Station, he got splashed by a passing cyclist. "Oh, no!" he yelled. "Now my pants are all wet!" To us Americans, that was a perfectly accurate observation—the lower half of his jeans was thoroughly soaked. To the Brits around us who all looked up in shock, however, this school-aged boy seemed to be declaring that he had just wet his underwear. The word "pants," you see, has a very different meaning on each side of the Atlantic.

What does that have to do with assumptions? Simple: misunderstanding. When you don't *know* what you are seeing (or saying!), you probably don't know what you are seeing (or saying).

A child who "goofs off" or is silly may actually be trying to avoid a task that is too hard or too long—one at which he knows he will fail or can't figure out how to begin. Another may talk endlessly about dogs because it's the topic on which she feels most comfortable, not because she wants to be a know-it-all. A cold and an allergy look very much alike. So can an NT child who is misbehaving and an Asperkid who is misunderstanding or frightened. That's why we have to match our responses to the circumstances, not the standards.

Most kids will tell you that lunch and recess (or for older kids, free periods) are their favorite parts of the school day. But for Asperkids, these are the worst, most anxiety-producing times of all. They're open-ended and unstructured. They're loud, scary, embarrassing and are anything but fun.

This year, I took up gardening. And I have to admit that I've been pretty excited to discover that I am not, in fact, instantly lethal to all plant life (which, after many attempts to care for the most basic of houseplants, I was pretty convinced was the case). While I wouldn't exactly say I have a "green thumb"—"chartreuse" might be fair.

That's why, when my mom, who was going to be traveling, asked me to take care of her aloe plant, I not only agreed, I even went so far as to repot "Al the Aloe" in a brand-new container as a surprise gift. I looked online, read that "Al" needed "bright light," and set "him" lovingly in a bright, sunny spot near my rose bushes. Only "Al" quickly began to wilt. And to then turn brown. And finally to look, well, really, really sick. There went my *Better Homes and Gardens* award. With little hope on the horizon, I went back to the gardening site I'd read and realized that I'd given "Al" "direct" light, when "bright" light was needed. They seemed pretty similar and I'd thought they were the same thing. It turns out, however, they are not.

And here is where we get to the topic of play; in particular, play among kids with Asperger Syndrome. All children negotiate the world through play. That's a given.

Play is how we learn to move, work, sort through information and react to those around us. As I wrote in *Asperkids: An Insider's Guide to Loving, Understanding, and Teaching Children with Asperger Syndrome*, it's how we practice "interpersonal connection, motor planning... conversational skills, cognitive and memory work" (Cook O'Toole 2012, p.67).

Play provides what children need to become functional adults. But, any given child on any given day has different skills that need developing. And like "Al the Aloe," if a child needs one set of circumstances and is provided with something else, he won't grow. He'll wilt.

Parents and teachers often notice that Asperkids play a little differently than typical children—what they don't realize is that's actually a good thing.

I have heard, "She has no imagination," from more than one parent describing their child (either disparagingly or woefully). But from where I stand, as an Aspergirl [myself] and mom to three Asperkids, I could not disagree more. (Cook O'Toole 2012, p.69)

Want proof?

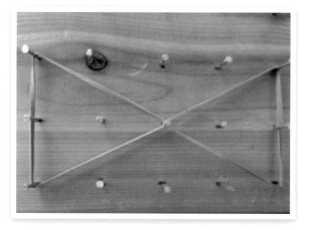

Here's a little sculpture my three-year-old made with rubber bands. When asked what it was, I guessed a butterfly? (Nope.) A bow-tie? (Nope.) It was, he said matter-of-factly, "a shout." I looked again—and there it was. Can you see it? Think of the way in which sound waves travel outward from one point...and it most certainly is a shout. Envisioned by a three-year-old. Now tell me that isn't imagination! Like other kids, Asperkids get what they need from play, too.

And since their needs are different, their play is different. They're seeking "bright" light, not "direct" light.

Shake It Up and Sort It Out

When my eldest Asperkid was about 18 months old, I got her a color and shape sorter. It had glossy, colored wooden pegs and brightly colored latex hearts, stars and circles, each with one smooth side and one textured side.

The objective was to fit the pieces onto the pegs either by color or by shape. And we'd begin, I decided, by sorting the colors. After a short demonstration, she caught on quickly, yet I noticed something strange. Without fail, my daughter made sure that those shapes were ALWAYS textured side up. If I'd flip one, she'd glare at me, and then switch it back.

A few months later, I decided to "shake up" the play by showing her that these little foam bits could also be sorted—ta-da—by shape! Giant mommy-smile on my face, I waited for a mirrored reaction. Instead, I got that stare again. "No," she emphatically said in her little toddler voice. "That's not right." And, with some ferocity, she proceeded to resort everything by color.

Textured side up.

To the mortal world, that might look like stubbornness. To those of us raising Asperkids, we recognize it as the precarious moment when we hold our breath—when our children get stuck on one idea (which to everyone else seems completely unimportant) and will NOT (or more fairly, *cannot*) move on without "fixing" whatever is amiss. Psychologists call it "rigid thinking" or cognitive inflexibility.

To Asperkids, there is only right or wrong answer, method or pattern—there is no "also possible." That's anxiety talking. And as an Aspie myself, I can only tell you that tolerating "also" can feel something like a pebble in your shoe. You can keep walking, but it's uncomfortable.

NT children enjoy spontaneous, "pointless" group play without much effort. And while Asperkids want friends, making and keeping them feels really hard. We all know that play is supposed to be fun. But to an Asperkid—whose mind naturally operates on logic-driven, if/then, concrete clarity—collaborative, open-ended group games aren't fun. They're really, really hard. So, they choose other kinds of play. Play that achieves what they need—and feels FUN to them. Here's the sneaky insider tip, though: Asperkids can still learn the interpersonal skills they need from the activities they enjoy. It just takes a little understanding of the hows and whys.

For example, one of the major challenges for Asperkids is something psychologists refer to as "theory of mind." That's fancy talk for being able to intuitively put yourself in someone else's place—to see their perspective, to imagine what he or she feels and thinks and to react accordingly. Without meaning to, they see the world as "me, and then everyone else" rather than "all of us together." They often have a hard time understanding that their own ideas, wants and beliefs aren't necessarily the same as everyone else's. That's why shouting, "I won! I won!" seems logical to an Asperkid—if she's happy that she's succeeded, shouldn't everyone be happy, too? But turn the situation around, and that same Asperkid may storm right out of the room if someone else succeeds.

At school, "mind blindness" makes group work hard. Working with a partner or team means being able to feed off of one another's input, to understand their perspectives and to explain your own. Young Asperkids who can't manage that well appear "bratty" or "bossy," sort of a "my way or no way" thing that teachers and peers won't like. As they get older, those Asperkids may either retain a "know-it-all" reputation (which they don't understand how they've created), or withdraw into solitary depression, or both.

That's why **it's up to us to remember** that their confusion, rigidity and anxiety come from a literal "blindness" to others' minds. It's not intentional; it's neurological. **And as parents, teachers or clinicians, WE adults have to be intentional in the way we use play to teach the skills they need.**

The other day, my daughter was playing a new brain-teaser book that she'd gotten as a reward for good deeds around the house.

I saddled up beside her, asked if I could join in—and got a big grin in return. "YES!" she agreed happily.

It's a universal fact that mothers just KNOW stuff. And this mother knew, after one quick look at the puzzle, that she was going to need a few visual tricks to help her negotiate the maze. Like many Asperkids, too much visual crowding can overwhelm her. And this momma knew that some simple tweaks (a highlighted number here, a colored box there) would be all she'd need to complete logic puzzles designed for kids much older than she.

Yet when I made my suggestions, she quickly became frustrated with me. She didn't need this idea or that marking. So I asked her to just let me try once—to humor me. With a (very loud) huff, she let me interfere…and immediately succeeded. Couldn't she just let me do it one more time? Fine, she relented…and she succeeded again. The fact is that none of us like to need help or to be wrong—that's pride talking. For kids who feel like total failures if they make a single mistake, that's even more true. But there is a BIG difference between appropriate accommodations and disempowering crutches. We do NOT want to create learned helplessness. We want to support appropriately—then stand back.

After she had finished a few puzzles, my daughter casually said, "Oh, go ahead. You can keep making the marks." Which I did, without comment—no "I told you so" or smug smile. What I did do, however, was bring it up later.

When presented as a concrete challenge where she was literally able to negotiate her way to her goal by accepting someone else's contribution, she was able to consider a much bigger and more abstract concept—

that not only is accepting help alright, it's smart. Sure, she could've done the puzzles without me, and yes, she got defensive when I tried to collaborate. But she learned, firsthand, that by accepting and eventually even inviting the input of someone who had her best interests in mind, she could make better use of her own talents and master the puzzle with less stress and more FUN.

And that's play with a purpose.

This Asperkid didn't learn about teamwork on a softball field or in a drama group. Maybe she will someday. For today, though, her puzzle was enough of an opportunity to learn that the best way to negotiate life's twists and turns is by listening to those who care, considering what they offer and then using your own talents to make your way through.

Like "Al the Aloe," Asperkids have their own set of needs to fulfill—it's not about right or wrong, it's about different. While my daughter didn't receive a "direct" getting-along-with-others tutorial on a crowded playground or classroom, it was a "bright" moment of understanding. And it was fun. So we'll keep playing with purpose and intention. And she, like "Al the Aloe," will bloom.

The Lesson of the Geocorona

During my career as both a social worker and as an educator, one fact has proven to be true over and over again: **approach is everything**.

Think of it this way. Earth is blanketed in an invisible ocean of gases which arrange themselves into layers. From the ground toward the sky, we'd find the troposphere, stratosphere, mesosphere, thermosphere and exosphere. Last, on the outermost edge of the exosphere, is the geocorona. It's nothing but a fuzzy, blue envelope of illumination—yet that border separates our fragile home from the vast dangers of space.

OK. Now imagine you are standing next to a pond with a stone in hand. Toss that rock at too steep an angle, and all you'll get is a splash where the water's surface shatters and a big kerplunk of protest from the disturbed molecules. Toss it "flat" (close to horizontal) and the stone will skip and bounce along.

The edge of our atmosphere behaves a lot like the water. When spacecraft reenter the earth's atmosphere, success depends on the approach. Too steep a pitch, and the craft will explode in a fiery ball. Too obtuse or "dull," and the ship will, like that stone, literally bounce off the exosphere and into space.

Safe passage requires just the right approach. That's true for a spacecraft getting through the atmosphere, a stone through the water, or an idea through personal defenses. Make a difficult point too sharply—be it academic, physical or social-emotional—and it will blow up disastrously. The human ego is a fragile thing, which doesn't like to be poked and pierced. On the other hand, subtlety will bounce right off personal "shields." Do not expect an Asperkid (or most people, for that matter) to absorb something simply because it seems "obvious." What is clear to one mind is unnoticed by another.

Speaking with the authority of an educator, a therapist and—most importantly—an Asperkid mom (× 3) with a "fully operational Asperkid kitchen lab," I assure you that even the most well-intended, wise, apt and insightful truth must be presented carefully if it is to reach the tender heart within.

In this book, you'll find necessary social and emotional concepts cloaked within spy games, origami geometry, trampoline hopscotch, optical illusion painting, fried marble jewelry-making, analogy scavenger hunts, molecular science cookies and even geode soap. It isn't fancy. It isn't complicated. It's fun. That's the approach.

What's the payload? Big stuff. Teamwork and flexible thinking. We'll consider multiple perspectives, learn coping strategies and identify feelings far beyond happy or sad. Meanwhile, there are clandestine fine motor work and visual closure practice. There's proprioceptive input and core academic standards like sorting and classifying, making analogies and discovering chemical change. In short, what lies ahead is the kind of play that Asperkids find FUN and we adults find rich with purpose.

Laying It Out

Intention. Direction. A game plan for life. Intrinsic to every success story is strategy—this is yours.

The Asperkid's Game Plan is a carefully arranged progression of projects, experiments and conversations designed for home, school and therapeutic use with all Asperkids (or any other kids, for that matter). Grounded in my professional work and personal insights, each project was *thoroughly* tested by my most honest (and most critical) "subjects"…my own three Asperkids. To make it past *them*, activities had to be different, FUN, interesting, FUN, original, and most of all, FUN. To make it past *me*, those same activities also had to effectively communicate complex ideas to very different young people.

Why? Because there's tough stuff to learn. In *The Asperkid's (Secret) Book of Social Rules* (Cook O'Toole 2013), I wrote about the many "hidden" expectations the world has that we Aspies simply miss. And, in the book's last section, "Practice Sessions," we go through a comic-style review of some of the newly introduced concepts.

So what comes after practice? The *Game Plan,* of course. And it's game time, folks, so let's play!

How Not to Make a Light Bulb

Why Everything is Hard Before It is Easy

From The Desk Of: Thomas Edison

Inventor's Notebook:

Method #894 on how NOT to make a light bulb.

Need-to-Knows

- Persistence means dedication even when you royally and publicly mess up.
- Skill develops over time, not overnight.

Each chapter in the *Game Plan* uses creative, entertaining play to (sneakily) practice specific social skills.

Here are the specific sets of primary psycho-social skills for each:

1. Anxiety management, logical (non-reactive) thinking, effective communication and flexible problem-solving.

2. Teamwork, collaboration and negotiation of roles.

3. Perspective-taking and impulsivity.

4. Part-to-whole relationships, inclusion and perception versus fact.

5. Cognitive flexibility, listening skills and theory of mind.

6. Absolutism, emotional awareness and emotional vocabulary.

7. Resistance to change, reciprocity and flexible thinking.

And a few more "need-to-knows" before you get started:

- Extension ideas make **every activity adaptable** to any age, ability or interest.

- **Academic and motor practice** are built into **every activity, with relevant** skills work highlighted at the start of each chapter.

- **Learning styles, component skills and areas of academic enrichment are listed for each themed chapter.**

For parents, explanations (or translations!) of those terms are given in the tables on the following pages.

C'mon, Already!

OK, it's time for your pep talk. Move right through the book from front to back, or skip around, addressing the social, academic or motor/sensorial need *du jour*. Remember to be clear, specific and consistent. Be curious and humble rather than sure and wrong. Don't assume. Take the time to ask, "Why?" Wonder. And above all—more important than any bullet point—have **fun.** Real life doesn't have any replays. Ready? Then come on. It's time to play!

Terms You're About to See
(Refreshers and "American Translations")
Learning Styles

People take in, understand and recall information in many different ways, which you'll sometimes hear described as "multiple intelligences." Whether the subject at hand is algebra, making compromises or setting the dinner table, matching teaching style and learning style ensures quicker success and greater self-esteem.

Here's a list of the learning styles you'll see accessed throughout the *Game Plan* and what they "look like" to an Asperkid:

Learning style	What that looks/sounds like in *real* life
Active	"Let's try it"—sitting still is difficult, as is listening attentively for a long time; likes to work in groups.
Reflective	"Let's think about it"—likes to work alone; needs time to digest information.
Sensing (BIGGIE among Asperkids)	Likes learning facts and using established methods, dislikes surprises; has difficulty with abstract, theoretical materials; good with details, memorizing facts and hands-on work.
Intuitive	Discovers possibilities and relationships; likes innovation, good at grasping new concepts; works quickly.
Visual	Learns best from what is seen.
Verbal	Learns best from use of words; will ask lots of questions about key vocabulary; often an avid reader and "grammar junkie."
Sequential	Learns best in logical steps/linear format.
Global	NOT an Asperkid first-pass (but good for review); sees the big picture and makes connections to prior knowledge.

Underlying Component Skills for Success

You'd never ask a toddler to run if he didn't know how to walk. And you'd never build the second story of a building without first constructing the ground floor. In school, at home and in general living, we are constantly layering new skills atop a foundation of established ones. But, if an underlying component is shaky, everything on top will be, too. That's why an occupational therapist knows that handwriting problems may actually indicate a visual processing deficit.

Component skill	Meaning
Attention	There are several types of attention skills, but all have to do with sustained focus.
Auditory motor integration	The integration of auditory skills and motor skills (rhythm). Example: tapping to a beat.
Auditory processing	The ability to process incoming auditory information quickly and accurately.
Bilateral coordination	The ability to use both sides of the body at the same time—for the same action (like using a rolling pin), using alternating movements (like climbing stairs), or for different actions, such as stabilizing a paper with one hand while writing with the other.
Cognitive	Relating to thinking, reasoning and/or remembering.
Emotional regulation	The ability to understand and accept an emotional experience, to use appropriate strategies to diffuse uncomfortable emotions and to continue to behave appropriately when distressed.
Fine motor	Fine motor control is the coordination of muscles, bones and nerves to produce small, precise movements.

Component skill	Meaning
Gross motor	Gross motor control is the coordination of the large muscles of the body for walking, running, sitting, crawling and other activities.
Language processing	Attaching meaning to sound groups that form words, sentences and stories.
Language skills	The ability to communicate effectively is a fundamental requirement of successful relationships, intellectual development and emotional satisfaction.
Motor planning	The ability of the brain to conceive of, organize and carry out a sequence of unfamiliar actions.
Oculomotor	The ability to use the eyes efficiently to read and gather information from the environment.
Problem-solving	The ability to handle and resolve traditionally and constructively any challenges, set backs, mistakes, failures or conflicts.
Processing speed	The ability to automatically and fluently perform relatively easy or practiced thinking tasks.

Component skill	Meaning
Sensory processing	The brain's blending and use of the information taken in through the body's senses.
Sequencing	The ability to arrange letters, words, numbers, ideas or tasks in a logical order.
Social skills	The interpersonal skills needed for successfully communicating and interacting with other people.
Visual auditory integration	The ability to match auditory and visual stimuli and coordinate them into a meaningful product.
Visual motor integration	The integration of auditory skills and motor skills (rhythm). Example: tapping to a beat.
Visual processing	The ability to make sense of information taken in through the eyes.
Visualization	The ability to recall an image of what has been seen and the ability to mentally manipulate and change aspects of that image in the mind.
Visual-verbal	The ability to receive information and ideas through listening and reading, and the ability to send or express information or ideas through speaking and writing.
Working memory	The ability to hold information in the mind while performing mental operation on it.

Academic Skills

These Core Standards are the common language used throughout the United States to describe particular academic skills. When you see the broad terms, you'll be able to tell which particulars are included.

Success (in life and in school) requires shoring up the complex network of foundational skills which underlie everything we do.

Broad category	Included skills
Language arts	Handwriting Reading—foundational skills Reading—information gathering Reading—literature Reading—range, quality, complexity Speaking and listening Spelling Writing
Mathematics	Counting and cardinality Expressions and equations Geometry Measurement and data Number and operations Operations and algebraic thinking Ratios and proportions Statistics and probability

Broad category	Included skills
Science	Asking questions Evaluating results Observation skills Testing hypotheses
Social studies	Health and fitness Involved citizens Productive workers Responsible family members Self-directed, lifelong learners

COLORED RICE, THREE DIMENSIONS AND SEE-THROUGH EGGSHELLS

The Foundational Role of Sensory Work

. . . .

Included Activities

1. That's My Name, Don't Wear It Out

2. Blindfolded Geometry and Communication Lessons

3. Expandable Hearts and See-Through Eggshells

    Snapshot-Sized Fun: Sort It Out!

    Snapshot-Sized Fun: Sensory Play to Go

    Snapshot-Sized Fun: Lost and Found

Primary psycho-social skills
Anxiety management
Effective communication
Flexible problem-solving
Logical (non-reactive) thinking

Motor and processing skills
Attention
Auditory processing
Bilateral coordination
Cognitive
Fine motor skills
Language processing
Motor planning
Problem solving
Sensory processing
Sequencing
Social skills (turn-taking)
Visual motor integration
Visual processing
Visualization
Visual–verbal
Working memory

Teaching/learning styles
Active
Auditory
Global
Intuitive
Kinesthetic
Reflective
Sensing
Sequential
Visual

Academic enrichment and reinforcement
Language arts (spelling, speaking and listening, writing)
Math
Science
Social studies

Some rice and food coloring. A bowl of popcorn kernels. A tub full of floral water beads. It's hard to believe, at first, that any of these are particularly important for anything other than preschool craft projects. But these tangible, explorable things actually invite some really sophisticated work. Real, "concrete" things that we see or smell or touch provide a bridge to discussions of more escoteric, "abstract" concepts. Beliefs. Emotions. Fears. Those things we each define and experience a little bit differently. Now, that's tough stuff for anyone, but it's really challenging for those of us on the spectrum. There's no impartial barometer to alert us

to emotional blunders. There's no gauge to verify what someone else means against what we perceive. So, we get confused. And hurt. And that's really no fun at all— as children or as adults. To give Asperkids (and autistic kids) a chance at success in the realms of the abstract, we must first introduce even the most intangible concepts via concrete experiences.

To put it simply, developing minds first learn through sensory input—it's our most primal method of absorption and observation. Knock into a block tower and it will fall. But sensory defensiveness, common in so many kids on the spectrum, can inhibit the creation of necessary learning foundations. So, encouraging a child to interact with more scents, sight, sounds and textures while just plain PLAYING (and messing around with volume, cause/effect and motor planning) will bring about more opportunities for conversation, self-regulation and higher-ordered thinking than you'd imagine. If you're too put off by the feel of rice, how can you fill up a funnel and watch gravity in action or figure out how to unclog the traffic jam of grains?

Socrates said, "That which is held in the hand is then held in the heart" (and, I would add, in the head). In order for a theoretical physicist to wonder about the impact of gravity on time distortion, he first has to see the stars with his own eyes. Concrete materials make concepts real, and therefore, easily internalized. In order for *any* child to develop deep foundational concepts, *concrete* hands-on learning materials are ideal; like no other method, sensorially-based, *real* beginnings optimize eventual comprehension of abstract concepts. Then, once those ideas are internalized, the "tangibles" (sandpaper letters, kinetic math materials and rearrangeable "constructive" triangles) are no longer necessary. But by first introducing language, math, geometry, history or science simply and concretely, we can cyclically present new degrees of abstraction and complexity as the child shows himself to be ready.

Spectrumites are capable of unparalleled abstraction, luscious creativity (Emily Dickinson), radically complex theory (Albert Einstein), mechanical tenacity (Henry Ford) and endearingly witty humor (Charles Schulz). It's just that our black/white, "show me don't tell me" minds REQUIRE the *independent* observation of patterns, trends and possibilities from REAL things, not from someone else's proclamations.

We on the spectrum live in a world that can feel terrifying in its random cruelty, uncertainty and inconsistency. That's why we are, so often, aggravated by changes in structure, routine and rules. We are not being obstinate for the sake of being obstinate. We are scared. And that is why, it seems to me, that the most difficult— but most important—thing for our loving families, friends, therapists and teachers to convince us of is that there is "more than one way to get to OK," whether that's folding towels, solving a math equation or packing a school bag.

That's where the genius of the sensory bin is born! With nothing more than an old sand and water table or dollar store storage bin, some fillers that you probably already have in your pantry and a little imagination, you can create fantastic treasure hunts that engage the senses and spark limitless curiosity at all levels of learning.

The basic recipe is simple: within a "filler" medium of your choice, bury items for the Asperkid to discover…and while you're at it, have some fun yourself. Get themey. Basic favorites—color, sports team or book—or something more high-brow, like examples of the Fibonacci sequence in nature. Almost anything goes for a central idea! For example try hiding objects that relate to:

- a holiday (candy canes, ribbon and evergreen for Christmas)

- a season (autumn leaves, acorns and pinecones)

- a special interest (Lego, model cars, "gems" and art supplies)

- a letter, letter sound or blend (see below)

- a concept (mathematics—sorting odd, evens, squared and cubed numbers, magnetism, geometrics, biomes, elements or even animal taxonomy).

Then, follow up with an "end cap" idea to provide a "finish line." Through sorting, matching or achieving a certain end, your Asperkid should be able to ascertain that the job is done and achieve a feeling of completion (but, of course, they can go back to the mess if they want).

We ALL need to be part of what we learn in order to truly understand it—whether that's grammar, cosmology, art, animal husbandry, weather patterns or social skills. To provide your spectrum kiddo with the countless practical, academic, physical, social and emotional skills that you MUST demonstrate, explain and repeat, be sure to provide every notion in a concrete, measurable and observable format. You, NTs, *can* learn that way. We, on the spectrum, *need* to learn that way, to communicate that way (through writing or art or construction) and to play that way. We can and will sing, leap, laugh and dream without limits; but, before we can venture into the conceptual, and the theoretical, before we can consider the abstract and *wonder*, we must stand squarely upon the "concrete"—and *know*.

Activity 1

THAT'S MY NAME, DON'T WEAR IT OUT

Ready, Set

Here's what you'll need:

- containers or storage tubs that are wider than they are deep—preferably clear plastic with a lid

- dry fillers (pick one and vary): rubber bands, birdseed, coffee beans, craft puffs, feathers, dried beans or pasta, popcorn or popcorn kernels, buttons, rice, pebbles or sand. OR:

- wet fillers: shaving cream, whipped dessert topping, water beads (from the floral section at craft stores), gelatin, wet sand, "insta-snow," or cooked noodles

- tools: magnifying glasses, spoons, funnels, tongs (various sizes); glass cups for measuring, manipulating, pouring and transferring; ice cube trays, small bowls, cups or cupcake liners for sorting.

Now, try to engage as many senses as possible—think of "coordinated music" (if you have a theme) or bells for sound, ribbons or shells for texture variation and even tiny mirrors or "jewels" for reflecting and refracting light. Don't forget scents! Add essential oils (rose, eucalyptus, vanilla or peppermint), dry spices (cloves, cinnamon or lavender buds), cupcake sprinkles and even baking mixes.

In this particular go, I also used household items that represented the sounds in my son's name.

Go!
G-A-V-I-N

Gavin has always loved puzzles—since, as he puts it, he was really little…but don't snicker. Playing is serious business.

Inspired by a favorite puzzle that spelled "G-A-V-I-N," this series of sensory bins began with an idea to assemble individual tubs containing items that corresponded with the letters in his name. However, when that turned out to be too easy, it wasn't hard to amp up the challenge as led by the child.

The first tub contained objects representing the hard "g" (to avoid confusion, so no "giraffe" here). I gathered a toy goat, a gear, a guinea pig puzzle piece, plastic glasses, a ghost-shaped cookie cutter and so on, finally submerging them all into the tub of bird seed. Cue ambience (singing "They Might Be Giants" and "Go for G!" on my iPod) and every letter "g" I could find for good measure. Then, the little guy went for it.

Using the scoops and a "g-lass," he dug around through the bits, pulling each discovery out and raising it high as he called out its name. Yet even here, there was an additional "sneaky" flexible thinking skill in play. "Present?" he asked, holding up a little plastic package and bow. "Does 'present' have a 'g'

sound?" I asked back, not leading one way or the other with my tone. "No," he scowled, and thought. He certainly knew the synonym in question, but word retrieval was stumping him. So, before he got too frustrated, I supplied, "We could also call it a gi…?" "Gift!" he finished triumphantly. He knew that every item had to begin with the same sound, so the "control of error" was built right into the game (alternatively, the child might have to sort out items which didn't belong).

The same thing happened the next day in our "a" (short "a" only) variation. He pulled a piece out and questioned, "Puzzle?" But that wasn't an "a." He tried, "Continent?" Closer, I assured him. "Africa!" And that was it. Happy dance!

So adept was he at this game that I decided to make it a bit more challenging the next day. Instead of one beginning sound, the objects could represent any of the three remaining letter sounds in his name: "v," short "i," or "n." He would determine which starting sound he heard and sort it into the correct letter group.

To help give visual structure to the length of the task (too big is too daunting!), I set out three papers, each one with one letter written in large block print AND in cursive (thereby helping him to link the concepts).

They would act like the check boxes do in a to-do list. I also listed in dot counters and in a numeral the amount of items to be sorted there, followed by a card that showed the outline of each correct object. He would have to dig for each treasure, decide which sound applied, find the correct letter category AND sit the object into the correct silhouette!

Now, we were involving sound discrimina-tion, letter and quantity comprehension, sorting and—hardest of all—the visual-spatial and fine motor skills to match an object with its general shape. (Note: I gave explicit instructions that having any object perfectly in the lines was NOT important so he wouldn't obsess and get stuck.) And just to make it extra fun, of course I had to have him run and jump and get in some good wiggle work, too!

Then the game was on! Would the noodle be a "v," "i," or "n"? Once decided, would it fit in the round spot (reserved for the base of a nutcracker) or the swirly spot? There were four places and we'd filled in three, so how many were left to be found? Which letter had the most items? Which one had the least? You could take the questions anywhere….and when he was all done, we arrived at the crowning moment. Taking the "g" puzzle piece from the first bin and each of the additional letters, Gavin filled in his "name puzzle" from beginning to end, utterly satisfied that he had mastered the challenge—and had a whole lot of fun along the way.

This activity very soon expanded to include miniature objects in rhyme families, and the letters that would spell each word—a tiny frying pan and a "p," "a," and "n," along with Spider M-A-N, a toy V-A-N, a B-A-G, a F-L-A-G, a tiny C-A-T, a Lego B-A-T and a doll's H-A-T, for example.

Fishing each item out with tongs, Gavin sorted the letters into a cupcake liner and the objects onto a tray. NEVER having attempted this before, we then divided up the word groups, with Mom constructing the ending sounds. Gavin would then pull the appropriate starting letters for each object and help me "build" each word in turn. He read every one. I'd mix the letters up, away from their objects, and he would do it again, completely independently. After all the words had been made, we scrambled the objects, and I drew three words out to the center. "Can you match the object to this word?" Out came the Lego bat to sit next to B-A-T, and so forth. By working to find and concretely construct language, he was reading and "writing" long before his motor skills would ever have allowed him to do the same.

And if this wasn't a face of utter self-satisfaction and triumph, I just don't know what would be.

Activity 2

BLINDFOLDED GEOMETRY AND COMMUNICATION LESSONS

Ready, Set

Here's what you'll need:

- a blindfold or scarf (if the Asperkid is comfortable with it)

- a bag

- solid objects in various geometric shapes: cube, sphere, cone, triangular prisms, rectangular prisms, pyramid, ovoid or ellipsoid

- four index cards, each marked with one of these qualifiers: size (in blue), shape (in red), pattern (green) and position (black)

- squares of felt or construction paper in the same color code.

- a sensory tub with dry filling.

Go!

How many senses do we have? Five, right? Well, not really. There's actually a sixth, called the stereognostic sense. You would probably recognize it better as "muscle memory," a blend of both touch and movement. If you break the word down, you can see that it's sort of a recipe, rather than an individual perception. Stereo refers to something's "solidness" and "three-dimensionality." Gnostic is having to do with knowledge. Put those together, and you can see the overall idea. Stereognostic sense is the understanding and ability to recognize the size, shape and proportions of an object using cues we take from its texture, weight, dimension and even its temperature. The information comes in through touch, yes, but the skill is how well we can correlate our tactile perceptions to visualization—to an accurate conception in our "mind's eye."

"What does this have to do with anything?" I can hear you thinking. I get it. Right off the bat, "stereognostic sense" sounds like a mouthful of pretty irrelevant jibber jabber. But it's not. It is the very mental and sensorial organization which, often underdeveloped in spectrum kids, can leave them feeling clumsy, disoriented and anxious. So, when working on sensory exploration, we have to be very sure not to leave out this forgotten "sixth sense."

That's what we did one afternoon with six-year-old Sean. Before we began the day's activities, we had a quick review of the solid geometric shapes he already knew and how they were related to plane (flat) shapes. He held a sphere, enjoying its wobbly roundness, and under supervision, sliced it in half, creating circle "stamps." He absorbed the feel of the sharp-edged triangular pyramid, determining that even a diagonal slice would still make a triangular plane shape (although a different sort of triangle).

With one finger, Sean traced angles and counted vertices, noting the breadth of a face versus the crease of its edges, then marking some with cotton swabs and paint so he could see them clearly, too. Then we talked it out: which shape had the most corners? Which had rounded surfaces? Were they all round? And then, we even drew a chart together (Aspies love visuals!), counting the faces, vertices and edges, and started talking about the similarities and differences.

From that chart, we noticed a really interesting pattern: if you added the faces and vertices of any of these shapes, you'd always end up with two more than the number of edges. This is actually a high-level concept called Euler's formula: $f + v = e + 2$…only in REALITY rather than in a textbook!

Our Table of Geometric Solids

Shape	Shape of base(s)	Number of faces	Number of edges	Number of vertices (corners)
CONE				
CUBE				
CYLINDER				
SPHERE				
RECTANGULAR PRISM				
RECTANGULAR PYRAMID				
TRIANGULAR PYRAMID				
TRIANGULAR PRISM				

"OK!" I smiled coyly, "Let's play 'Who Am I?'" Sean would use our chart for reference, and I'd ask, "I have one circular face and one curved surface. Who am I?" (A cone.) Or, "I have six faces which are all congruent. My edges are also all congruent, and I have eight vertices altogether. Who am I?" (A cube.) Then, we'd mix it up: Sean would give clues and I would have to guess.

And so the game was already involving sorting, classification, comparative *and* descriptive skills. Lining them all up, I asked what the ovoid, ellipsoid and sphere had in common?

Now, understand, this is complicated—but not because of the geometric terminology. It's the behind-the-scenes work that's tough; the hidden-skill-upon-hidden-skill layering that so many teachers and parents don't realize they are asking their Asperkids to simultaneously perform. That single question asks the child to assess what he sees and feels, to detect some pattern among the specified objects *and* then to recall the words he would need to communicate that pattern thoroughly and clearly. That is a *lot* happening in what seems like a very simple task.

What may look like not understanding a math concept is, for example, just a glitch in communication. Ideas come out in a disjointed way. Non-essential questions are asked and re-asked. And frequently, reading comprehension and expressive language challenges (spoken and written) have nothing to do with vocabulary or accurate word attack. Those missing story details, vague summaries and forgotten connections are symptoms of being on the spectrum—of being a bit stuck in our own minds. **The challenge is not academic. It's psychological.** It is very hard for Aspies to visualize and then verbalize…to connect abstract—written or spoken words and thoughts—with concrete things. No amount of remedial schoolwork is going to change that; it will merely wound fragile egos and derail self-confidence. **The key is to give concrete foundations, and then reminders, for every abstract.**

The onus is on us—the grown-ups—to take the time to look, question and be keenly aware of which "ingredients" go into every task we require. Knowing all of this, it was my responsibility to establish my son's initial success. First, providing information from which he could choose, rather than requiring him to supply it. So, I could say and/or write down the possibilities, to help him remember the options while considering them. "Are all of the figures: polygons?" (have him look), "two-dimensional?" (have him look), "curvilinear?" (have him look), "or prisms?" (have him look).

Why all the looking? **Because at a certain point (every individual's threshold is unique), your Asperkid won't be able to listen to, remember and consider all of her options and choose or repeat the best one.** Aspies (adults and kids alike) can't rely on our working memory for the answers to most things. We need checklists, to-do lists, alarms and reminders. In school, Asperkids have to take the time to go back to the text and check their answer. In life, we have to practice reflective listening, being sure that what we heard and what was actually said (and meant) match. And you can begin it all with shapes (but don't worry— it gets more exciting!).

For example, start with a simple picture, like:

Ask, "Are all the figures the same color? The same size? Facing the same direction? Semi-circles?" Just increase the challenge with patterns and directionality if that's too easy.

Show an illustration like this one—"Are they all quadrilaterals? All blue? Congruent?" Advance the complexity, classifying by multiple characteristics. Put out four index cards, each marked with one of these qualifiers: size (in blue), shape (in red), pattern (green) and position (black).

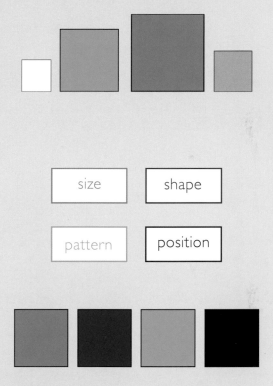

Together, and then independently, can he tell which are the same or different? Encourage your Asperkid to touch the cards one at a time, and name the characteristics of the objects they see. For the next round, flip the index cards over so only an "s," "s," "p" or "p" shows as a reminder—but use the same color codes.

Over time, your Asperkid will be able to independently generate her own cohesive sentences. To get there, swap out the cards for squares of felt or construction paper in the same color code—no words, just the colors.

Touching (and eventually just looking at) each square gives a concrete reference point for each idea they need to visualize and verbalize. For example: "The objects are in a row (position) and are all quadrilaterals (shape), but they are each a different color (pattern/color) and size."

Shapes are only a starting point. Your best bet for engaging an Asperkid is *always* via their special interest, especially if something is hard. For example, Sean is presently fascinated with the American presidency. After he had felt his geometric shapes, we looked through some of his favorite picture books for Abraham Lincoln's log cabin (a rectangular prism) and the cylindrical columns at the White House. Then, I'd ask him to tell me about what he saw—without me looking. I'd repeat back, "OK, you're making me see…" and a lot of times, he would realize that what he said wasn't as complete or clear as it needed to be.

Folks, trust me on this. I'm an author and speaker. Writing and teaching are what I do for a living—so I *have* to be able to absorb information, mull it around, and then effectively communicate my original ideas if I'm going to be able to entertain and educate you. Within the confines of my own head, I have always been able to take in, consider and opine. And I've always loved to write. But I clearly remember in high school when my English teacher handed back an essay (which I was *sure* was fantastic) and told me to rewrite the whole thing. The only problem was that she didn't explain what was wrong in a way that I understood. All she said was, "You're making the reader do all the work." What? I'd written a whole essay, and the reader was doing work? To me, that made no sense at all.

Decades later, I finally "get" what she meant (which says to me that *she* certainly wasn't doing a whole lot of work 20 years ago!). Today, Sean looks at a scene of his presidents, thinks a blazingly fast, probably crazily insightful string of ideas yet only communicates in disconnected pieces. There's Point A. And there's Point B. And even Point C. But I have no idea what has taken us from one to the other. **Living with an Asperkid often feels like one giant non sequitur—random thoughts that don't seem to have any logical relationship to anything else that's happening.** Of course, if you are the one speaking, everything makes sense. Every connection made within your own mind is pretty darned logical, and as an Aspie, feels obvious—as though the world can read your mind and already knows everything you're thinking. **Stopping to actually explain every step from A to B seems unnecessary and often, to be honest, doesn't even occur to Aspies.**

This was my trouble in my writing. I'd cite the perfect few sentences from the novel I'd read, yet never really say why they were there, what I thought they meant, or why they particularly mattered. So when my teacher said I was making the reader do all of the work, what she meant was that because I wasn't clearly and thoroughly communicating my ideas and connections, the reader was left trying to figure out the relevance of my citations and how I had arrived at my conclusions. The issue was never my reading or my writing. It was all Aspie you-mean-you-can't-see-my-thoughts communication meltdown.

When an Asperkid is asked to identify why this is a cone and that's a pyramid, to explain the significance of a world event or evaluate how one person is a better friend than another, she must observe, assess, classify, compare/contrast, recall, compose and convey a mountain of information. So, we have to go first. We can't read their minds, but they can't read ours, either. **We have to tell Asperkids what they need to tell us.**

Offer these keywords to your Asperkid as reminders when describing *anything*, be it their day, setting a scene in a story, comparing current events—anything. Beyond "s," "s," "p" or "p," these are the inclusive characteristics that will help your Asperkid thoroughly visualize their own ideas and then explicitly and completely communicate those thoughts to those of us who so want to hear them.

Stop. Notice. Describe:

- what (the subject)

- who (names, ages and gender)

- when (era and time of day)

- number (quantity)

- color

- shape

- size

- where (location)

- movement (speed, type and direction)

- mood

- background

- perspective

- sounds

- lighting.

Practice describing an illustration of his favorite dinosaur or of her favorite medieval portrait: use what is interesting, use visual cues to maintain focus and spark memory (like colored felt or paper with these words and, eventually, without) and repeat back "You're making me see…" Last, ACKNOWLEDGE every time you hear your Asperkid providing one of those key descriptors. It's as simple as saying, "You painted such a clear picture in my mind," or "That was great how you made note of…" If you want better communication, communicate better.

These skills are multi-layered and develop over time, so be patient, but get working. You can begin just as Sean and I began…playing with blocks.

After we had explored his solid shapes thoroughly and talked them over as well, Sean sat down and slipped on a soft blindfold (although an uneasy player could simply close his eyes).

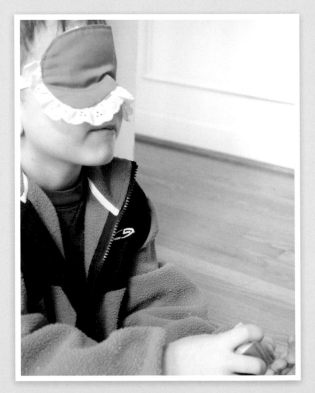

The wooden solids went into a cloth bag, and visualizing, verbalizing and stereognostic skills were engaged! It was the moment of truth: by touch alone, could he still identify each shape *and* remember the names? Absolutely. He could even tell me why this was a cube but that was a rectangular prism. Bam!

Sure of himself, Sean took off the blindfold and then laid out cards that named and illustrated each of the solid shapes. We were off to the sensory bin! Strewn amongst colored rice were 25 real-world spheres (balls and marbles), cubes (an origami box), prisms (jars and tiny boxes) and such, gathered from all about the house. Sean dug around, pouring and scooping and poking as he went, and eventually found all 25 objects. Then, he categorized the discoveries by matching each to the correct label card.

After he finished, I explained that there was one last shape to find. He looked again at the bin. Nope, nothing in there! However, I smiled, there were "spheres on top of cones in the freezer."

A pause and then, "You mean ice cream cones?" he asked. YES! Sweet. And serious game win.

Activity 3

EXPANDABLE HEARTS AND SEE-THROUGH EGGSHELLS

Ready, Set

Here's what you'll need:

- two eggs (plus a few spare ones to experiment with!)

- white vinegar

- dark corn syrup

- six glasses

- a kitchen scale

- gummy bears.

Go!

Older kids love sensory bins, too (heck, even adults get lost in letting the grains run through their fingers!). The key is to tie the materials themselves into more sophisticated concepts… and for a tween or teen, a particularly important topic of discussion is how the people and ideas around us can lift us up or drag us down. But you can't jump right in to "emotionally touchy" stuff without some serious eye-rolling. So, get "touchy" in a completely different way: raw, goopey and gucky eggs. Cracking a few together and practicing the gentle pull-apart motion needed to open the shell, ten-year-old Maura and I let the runny whites and fatty yolk drip through our hands. Gross? Yes. Fun? YES!

"Look there," I stopped her, mid-muck. "See? Beyond the fragile shell, is an even more fragile, paper-thin membrane." Maura was amazed by the intricate, lace-like patterns webbing the translucent skin and wondered aloud how she'd never noticed it before.

"That's true for a lot of things we see often," I said casually. "The more mundane something seems, the less attention we give it." It was, we agreed, sort of like never seeing the sites in your own city, but all the tourists have been.

"But, back to the egg," I said. "How do you suppose the chick breathed while it was inside?" Sean piped up (as younger brothers will) that there were actually really tiny holes in the surface of the shell which allowed gas, like air, to pass through it. "Yes, that's it. Even though it's solid, an eggshell is gas-permeable" (I repeated the word a few times), "or penetrable, a boundary that gases can easily cross."

"What about other things, like liquids?" I mused. "If you poured water on the shell, would it leak in?" "No, of course not." They said. " If you boil eggs, after all, they don't soak up the cooking water." "Well, what about the membrane? Is it liquid-permeable?" I asked. They weren't sure. After all, there was no way to test *just* membrane with no shell. So, you couldn't really tell if one or both were keeping the water out…or could you?

I called the boys over and asked them to hold a paper towel stretched between them. On cue, Maura poured a cup of water onto the towel, and as they predicted, liquid seeped through the porous fibers.

Then, we made a change, spilling water out onto a sheet of aluminum foil—the water pooled, immobile.

One solid was liquid-permeable, they decided. The other was most definitely not.

As we cleaned up the mess, I pushed a bit more… off-handedly. "So, the whole permeability thing. It kind of reminds me of people," I said. Maura looked at me quizzically, and I continued, not looking at her directly. Her school had just finished a year-long immersion project in which they had visited with legislators and factory workers, investigated the workings of personal and public economy and then recreated what they had observed by founding their own city (from currency to taxes and even working industries). Maura herself had been a "city councilwoman"

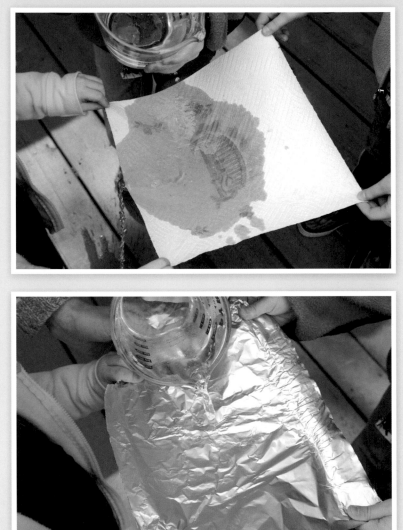

(which my mother actually was in real-life), so she had developed a rather personal relationship with government sticking points. I planned on using that.

"Take, for example, politics," I started aloud. "You could have the best lawmakers in the world with the best intentions in the world, but if they show up to work completely unwilling to listen or learn—if they are completely impermeable—there's no peace and prosperity, there's just instant quagmire and bureaucracy." "That makes sense," she agreed. "On the other hand," I continued, "everyone needs boundaries, both for their bodies and minds. We all start out, or should with adults as benevolent 'dictators,' teaching us how far is too far, what's safe and what's not. Eventually, we each have to take on the job for ourselves. That's maturity. Remaining totally 'permeable'—open without discretion—to *every* influence, idea and fad leaves us very vulnerable to predators of all sorts. There is a saying I remember; 'If you don't know what you stand for, you'll fall for anything.' Somewhere in the middle—semi-permeable—is probably best." She seemed to consider.

"Anyway," I interjected, changing topics before I could get preachy, "let's get the vinegar." And we turned back to the eggs.

The kids had, correctly, figured out that you couldn't test the egg's membrane with the shell in tact. But if you got rid of the shell, they'd agreed, the membrane would tear. Or would it? "Maura," I smiled. "We are now going to make naked eggs."

Each of the two eggs went gently into a glass and were then covered with white vinegar. "An eggshell," I explained, "is made of calcium carbonate—basically, calcium and carbon. As soon as we add the vinegar, some of the shells' chemical bonds will dissolve immediately, and…ta da!" Right on cue, carbon dioxide bubbles appeared as the shells began to disintegrate. We left them alone and in just a day or so, there was a white powdery residue on the glass. What was it? The calcium from the eggshell! The same stuff that made up our teeth and bones.

Our eggs remained in their baths for a week, carefully maintained with enough vinegar to keep them covered. After seven days, Maura was allowed to carefully lift the first egg, gently rubbing it smooth—and there, in her hand, was a naked egg. A bright yellow egg yolk floating within its liquid whites, held together by a rubbery membrane and completely devoid of that pesky shell. The second egg was identical.

And now what? Now, we weighed each "naked" egg and recorded the information. Two clean glasses were set out: one filled with plain water and the other with dark, viscous corn syrup. One egg went into each and we walked away for one day.

The next afternoon, I called the boys in to join us. All three kids were asked to follow me into our downstairs half-bathroom where, as you might imagine, we were completely squished when packed in together. "Welcome to a concentrated solution," I announced. "You are now a molecule. And it's tight in here. Is anybody happy?" Definitely not. Without a word of direction, I opened the door…and instantly, they walked out. "Very good, young molecules," I called from behind. They looked back. Huh?

Molecules. Kids. It didn't matter. Nature likes balance. If you're cramped and you see a way to get more room—less squished—you just naturally take it. No one had said, "Walk out of the room now." It's natural to want to move from a crowded place to one that's less jammed. Molecules do the same thing. They'd rather have everything all evened out—to be in equilibrium—than be smooshed. And then I brought them to the glasses.

The first egg had been placed in water. Very carefully, Maura lifted it out of the glass— and before she even weighed it, she could see what had happened. Without its shell, the liquid most certainly *did* get inside. Our little egg had ballooned up! The other egg, however, had been placed in corn syrup, and it looked pitiful.

Surrounded by a denser (hypertonic) area, the egg's original water content had passed out, trying to "equal" things out. In fact, Maura noticed, she could even see an inch or so of water floating on top of the corn syrup! All that was left behind in the membrane were the fats and proteins that were too big to get through the membrane.

It should probably be noted that for the sake of that all-important factor, fun, there were a few other objects left to soak overnight: gummy bears. Some gummy bears took the plunge in water, others bathed in salt water. And, just like the eggs, those in the hypotonic solution got HUGE, while the others shrunk like some poor taxidermy project gone wrong. The rest of the bag? Well, a girl's gotta eat.

While that particular girl (Maura, not me), enjoyed her gummies, I brought out the key to her more sophisticated sensory tub. Unlike her brothers, who were looking for items within the filler, the discovery for Maura was the very filler material itself—floral "water beads."

Starting out as teeny, glasslike balls, the beads would, like the egg, undergo a dramatic physical change when put into water. Osmosis would expand their size hundreds of times over right in front of her eyes.

Yes, of course, she loved the cool, slippery feel, but just as much, she loved understanding what happened and why…knowing that the hypotonic solution flooded into the tiny spheres, then measuring the difference and finally, determining the percentage of change in mass…yet there was more to talk about, later on. The tangible visual of the expanded egg yolk and membrane was really a metaphor for what I most wanted for this girl on the brink of adolescence: **we come into this world with gifts and buoyant spirits—like the "naked"** eggs, we are resilient, yet terribly fragile. If we submerge ourselves in an environment that is dark and clingy, like the thick, sticky syrup, we wither. We deflate. We become much, much less.

On the other hand, like the influx of the surrounding water into the egg, the right teachers, friends and loved ones cause us to grow and stretch…if we, like the permeable membrane, allow outside perspectives to enter. Our greatest ideas and talents also expand when enveloped in kind, gentle and intelligent relationships. It's the diffusion of imagination and creativity. We open ourselves by being "permeable," not rigid or unyielding, for a hard "shell" prevents others' gifts from reaching us…and our gifts from flowing out into the larger world.

So, was this a bonanza of eggy, wet and vinegar-scented sensory exploration? You bet. And along the way, more than a little bit of "awesome," too.

Snapshot-Sized Fun

SORT IT OUT!

Ready, Set
Here's what you'll need:

- blank index cards

- a pile of geometric solid blocks, ordinary household items in those shapes (like a soup can or tennis ball), or sketches of the shapes from the table on page 44.

Go!

- Copy each of the Surfaces characteristics from the following page onto an index card or piece of paper, and put them into a pile, face down. Or better yet—generate your own lists WITH the players!

- Do the same with the Edges and Corners characteristics.

- In turn, each player chooses and flips over a Surfaces card and an Edges and Corners card. They must then try to select a shape that fits both descriptions.

- Challenges are allowed once the kids are sure of themselves.

- "Steals" are also allowed if a player says that none of the shapes in the pile can be used, but another player sees a solution.

- If you run out of shapes before you run out of cards, continue the game. Players may "steal" from one another if someone else's object fits another pair of characteristics.

- The winner is the person who ends up with the most shapes in his or her personal cache.

Note: these "cards" describe a cone, cube, cylinder, sphere, rectangular prism, triangular prism, triangular pyramid and rectangular pyramid. You can also play this with 2D shapes.

Surfaces Characteristics

I have one curved surface.	I only have one surface.	I have three flat surfaces.
I have no flat surfaces.	I have an even number of surfaces.	All of my surfaces are flat.
I have two flat surfaces.	I have an odd number of surfaces.	My base surface is square.
I have both a curved and a flat surface.	I have both a curved and a flat surface.	My base surface is a circle.

Edges and Corners Characteristics

All of my angles are right angles.	I have no edges.	Three edges meet at one of my corners.	Two (or more) of my edges are perpendicular.
My bases are both flat.	I have one base.	All of the edges that connect my bases are parallel.	I have an odd number of corners.
I only have one vertex (corner).	I have an even number of edges.	I have an even number of corners.	I only have curved edges.
I have no vertices (corners).	All of my edges are straight lines.	An even number of edges meet at one of my corners.	WILD CARD (anything goes!)

Snapshot-Sized Fun

SENSORY PLAY TO GO

Ready, Set
Create your own "lava lamp" and take the sensory fun in the car, on the plane or bring it along for boring waiting rooms.

Here's what you'll need:

- large zip-top plastic bag AND duct or packing tape

- filler: glowing water (see our recipe on page 124), body wash, hair gel, lotion, shaving cream, bubble solution, oil (light-colored/clear baby or vegetable)

- objects: glitter, foil, confetti, and/or food coloring.

Go!

1. Put the filler into the bag and then choose a theme for the "objects" you'll add.

2. Toss in anything you'd like!
   For example:

   - see-through window-cling letters, shapes or holiday decorations

   - marbles

   - buttons

- shells and sand

- mini-erasers.

3. Gently close the bag, smoothing out remaining air as you do. Reinforce the closed top with the packaging tape. Then squish, hunt, discover and play!

Bag themes are limitless:

- foreign language vocabulary practice (counting/naming objects or their colors)

- special interest or favorite-book-related

- ecosystems

- animal classifications

- geography (cities, countries or even oceans)

- seasons or holidays

- mini-objects and the letters that spell their names

- water beads (include lots for easy addition, subtraction, multiplication practice!)

- droplets of colored water in oil.

Snapshot-Sized Fun

LOST AND FOUND

Ready, Set

"I Spy" takes on a homemade twist in these personalized, portable versions. Here's what you'll need:

- dry filler as used in sensory bins

- an empty, clear bottle

- objects to hide.

Go!
Version 1

1. Fill the bottle by alternately layering objects and filler.

2. Leave about an inch of open space between the fill line and the bottle top.

3. Put the cap on tightly!

4. Roll, flip and spin the bottle around until all the objects are found.

Version 2

1. Make a list of the objects to be found.

2. Crowd the objects into a baking casserole.

3. Now add distractions: anything from toy cars to coins to hardy candy.

4. Be sure that ALL the "must finds" are visible.

5. Take a photo, zoom in (enlarge) and print out.

6. Challenge players to find all of the objects within the photo.

7. You can make an entire binder or folder-full of these images to take on a long trip!

You can use look-and-find games in LOTS of ways:

- to connect with your Asperkid by hiding items that relate to her special interest

- to challenge him to detect phonemic patterns between miniatures (e.g. toy sheep, jeep, cheese, train, chain and brain)

- to help your Asperkid create an "All-About-You" gift by asking her to name things that *someone else likes* (a great theory of mind exercise).

Chapter 2

HUMAN KNOTS AND CAKE

What it Means to Be Part of a Team

. . . .

Included Activities

1. The Tray of Randomness

2. The Human Knot

3. Lego My Creation!

4. Gaming: Extra Tips for Everyone

   Snapshot-Sized Fun: Where Do I Fit In?

Primary psycho-social skills
Collaboration
Negotiation of roles
Teamwork

Motor and processing skills
Attention
Auditory motor
Auditory processing
Bilateral coordination
Cognitive
Emotional regulation
Fine motor
Language
Language processing
Motor planning
Problem-solving
Sensory processing
Sequencing
Social skills
Visual processing
Visual verbal
Visual-auditory integration
Visualization
Working memory

Teaching/learning styles
Active
Auditory
Global
Intuitive
Kinesthetic
Reflective
Sensing
Sequential
Visual

Academic enrichment and reinforcement
Language arts (speaking, listening and writing)
Math
Science
Social studies

When our eldest was little, she was in the hospital a lot. That stinks, no matter how you dress it up. While we couldn't change the facts, we could make sure she knew that we would always be with her through every moment, no matter how upsetting or scary. She was the one in the hospital gown, yes, although she wore it as part of a team: "Team O'Toole." We would share the burdens, decisions and uncertainty, and together, become just a little bit stronger than we ever would have been on our own. It was one heck of a way to learn the meaning of "team," that's for sure. But without realizing it, by creating "Team O'Toole," we had inadvertently created a lifelong reference point for our kids.

Honest truth: in general, the concept of being part of an all-for-one-and-one-for-all "team" is rather unnatural to most Aspies. The exception, I suppose, would be a team where each member has very clearcut duties that don't overlap (which is really more "parallel work" than teamwork). Why? Aspies (of all ages) have inherent difficulties understanding other people's wants and needs, a penchant for misinterpreting others' words and actions and, thanks mostly to anxiety, we're often in greater need of explicit validation. To put it simply: group work just isn't our natural thing.

Usually, you'll spot Asperkids craving control and affirmation or retreating to largely inconspicuous sideline (or even backstage) roles. And all of this makes sense. As leaders, Asperkids get to avoid the difficulties of give-and-take in peer negotiation. They can avoid the disappointments inherent to compromise and allow their brilliant minds to steamroll forward (even if they don't manage it with fantastic interpersonal success). On the sidelines, they don't attract much attention and thus avoid the criticism or rejection of not being wanted by their peers. It's no surprise then, that Asperkids, as a whole, much prefer school projects, sports activities and career choices where success isn't reliant upon others' input.

So why make a big deal about learning the "team" thing? Simple. Teams are everywhere, and they don't require uniforms. Friendships. Lab partners. Scouting troop members. Siblings assigned a chore together. Spouses. Each and every one is a team whose members must CONSTANTLY communicate, determine and verify what they are doing and how they are doing it.

OK, then, what exactly is teamwork? I say it's understanding common goals, staying actively committed to those goals and navigating shared loss and success.

It's not part of an Aspie's natural hard-wiring. And it won't come about through wishful thinking. For an Asperkid to have a successful marriage, family life (now and later) and meaningful friendships, we adults have to intentionally (and kindly) teach the experience of being on a team. So we begin with your team: the family.

How to start? First, you need a clear, common definition. In other words, exactly what is a team, and what does a team need to be successful?

Activity 1

THE TRAY OF RANDOMNESS

Ready, Set

Here's what you'll need:

- two large trays, cake pan, measuring cups and oven

- flour, baking powder, milk, eggs, vanilla, butter and sugar, all in their containers.

Go!

Without explanation, the experiment began by gathering the would-be team (in this case, the family, but it could also be a class, club or therapy group) together. There, I had already laid out a tray with vanilla, flour, eggs, butter, sugar, milk and baking powder. What, I asked, did they see? Everyone shrugged. "A lot of kitchen things?" suggested Gavin. Sean began listing each item in turn, giving us a complete run-down. Last, Maura, who has the world's largest sweet tooth, saw a convenient connection: "Baking stuff!"

This had to be their deduction to make, with the adult as a mere directress. A nod of consideration and a smile told them I was listening, but I offered no opinions or commentary. Next, I dealt out the ingredients like playing cards, asking each person to announce his lot. Flour and eggs here, milk and baking soda there. It still sounded like a grocery list.

"Maybe," I suggested, "we'll use the eggs to make an omelet and use the milk for my coffee. Or maybe we'll keep them separate, doing their own thing. Maybe the vanilla is just here to smell lovely and maybe the milk is for cereal."

Then the group laid each ingredient in a long, disconnected line. "Right now," I asked, "we could say that all of these random things are close together. True?" Agreement. "But are they connected? Joined in any way—other than Maura's hope for baking?" Nope. From eggs to flour, each was separate and in its own container. There was no mixing, no blending. They were a group of individual things. Or, to use Maura's words, "a whole bunch of random stuff

sitting there on the tray not doing anything." That's about right. A "group" doesn't get much done at all.

"But can't we bake something?" asked the sugar-lover desperately. "We could put them all together and make…well, something yummy!" And there she had it. A group is missing one very important ingredient: purpose. Unify the disconnected pieces toward a common target, and the group evolves into something new…a team. Our pantry goods needed a purpose (like dessert!) to become anything more than a tray of randomness. "So, what purpose should we give this group to make it a team?" I asked. And the resounding (not particularly surprising) answer? "LET'S MAKE 'TEAM CAKE'!"

Frantic measuring, pouring, mixing and baking immediately ensued. An hour later, when the room was quiet, mouths stuffed with sweet yumminess, I asked again about the original "group" of things on the tray. When, exactly, had they gone from "random" and "pointless" to exciting? Sean's description was the best: "When the ingredients 'joined forces,' they became a team." It was kind of like the Justice League or the Avengers—each individual is fine on his own, but put everything all together, and you have epic coolness.

As a team, we had concluded our own definition *of* a team: a group that works together to reach common goals. So, what about *our* team? What were our common goals? Everyone had opinions to add (loudly), and in the end, the list was whittled down to: safety, love, respect and kindness. Wonderful. Laudable. Estimable. But.

What about when life "divides and conquers?" What would happen when one Asperkid lost on family game night? Or if another's plans got changed at the last minute? What then? How would they stay focused on the common goals when feeling angry, disappointed or just plain grouchy? What then?

Suddenly, those crumb-laden faces looked more than a little bit worried. (However, the next game plan AND this list of "Simple Steps to Successful Teamwork" were already well-prepared.)

Simple Steps to Successful Teamwork

1. State your "FOR RIGHT NOW" goals.

   BEFORE MOVING ON: the TEAM must agree on common, clear, specific GOALS.

2. Share all instructions/information/background with the group.

   BEFORE MOVING ON: Ask, is there any information that hasn't been shown to ALL members? Do we all have the same facts?

3. Take turns sharing individual impressions, observations, feelings, questions.

   BEFORE MOVING ON: Reflect back what each person is saying to be certain that what is understood matches up with what is intended. Ask for clarification whenever needed.

4. Check if everyone is ready to move on to action!

5. Suggest solutions that will help achieve your common goals. Listen to one another with patience and respect. Be willing to try others' ideas.

6. Verify each member's responsibilities and agree on the time frame for completing the tasks. Decide when the group will gather again.

7. Break! Do your part and stick to the plan the TEAM has agreed upon.

8. Share progress and obstacles in real time.

9. Reunite to review the project.

10. Have the TEAM's goals been achieved? What went well? What could've been better?

Activity 2

THE HUMAN KNOT

Q: What do you think is our team's most important "to do" today?

Four-year-old Gavin: "I just can't figure it out yet. I can't say what I think. Lego, probably."

Seven-year-old Sean: "Playing! And Monopoly."

Ten-year-old Maura: "Alone time. Reading."

John (aka, Dad): "Getting your car inspected. It's overdue."

Me: "Collecting tax receipts and refilling prescriptions."

We may be a team, and we may say that we have common goals, but day-to-day life reveals very different priorities. So how do you help Asperkids go from "lip service" to walking the walk? How do we build the team we want them to experience?

A team has common goals, we agreed. Yet in our answers, we clearly saw that teammates' priorities don't always match. So we needed to hone our focus (a little bit artificially) onto a single task. Enter…The Human Knot. You may have tried a team-building game like this somewhere along the line, but adding varying heights, ages and personalities can make it a whole new shebang.

Ready, Set, Go!

- Have everyone stand in a close circle, facing one another. The more people you have, the better.

- Next, each person extends his hands into the middle of the circle, randomly grasping a different child's hand in each of his own.

- Now go at it! Climb under and step over each other; spin around, twist through, straighten out your knot, laugh at your oh-so-graceful selves, and NEVER let go of one another.

You've got the common, simplified goal down now: solve the problem without breaking up the team. But more than anything else, it's **CLEAR communication—carefully explained and double-checked ideas—which most determines whether a team will succeed.** After all, if we don't clearly share our concepts, plans or expectations, or if we don't verify that we've understood our teammates' messages, how can we be sure we're still operating toward the same goal? Simple answer: we can't be.

Good communication takes reflection, introspection and deliberate effort. Yet for us Aspies, we easily forget that other people cannot read our minds or know our hearts unless we explain ourselves very clearly. Our perspectives, our priorities seem to us like "no brainers," no-alternative conclusions, obvious and universal and certainly not requiring explanation. Oftentimes, I admit, I can't imagine that there are ideas in my head or notions in my heart that everyone else can't already KNOW just by looking at me. My mind, my heart and my "plan" each feel utterly transparent.

On the flip-side, you all may as well be made of lead. Unless you take the time to logically and clearly explain yourselves, we can't (not won't, CAN'T) anticipate your priorities and plans, even though you often expect that we will.

For example, Mom can't assume that her Asperkid "gets" the import of *her* "have-to-dos"—like a necessary stop at the grocery store or run for a prescription before the shop closes—if she hasn't explained them well. These "have-to-dos" don't feel urgent to the Asperkid at all! However, the game she'd PROMISED to play after school is *obviously* extremely urgent! Like the uninterrupted shower you've missed, he's been looking forward to that "together" game time all day!

The same would be true if tonight is Tuesday Taco Night and suddenly, Dad brings home pizza. Mom is thrilled (she has a headache and doesn't want to cook), but the Asperkid wants the promised tacos! What does a headache have to do with breaking a promise? Priorities, people!

In all seriousness, though, this isn't a kid who means to be self-centered or rude. NTs see egocentrism where there is, in fact, anxiety, upheaval and loneliness. Order, plans, routines, promises—they mean safety. Disruption, on the other hand, feels scary and chaotic. That's why making schedule changes without giving an Asperkid prep time (though that's real life!) feels disrespectful…even mean.

To an Asperkid, it's as if everyone's ganging up on you, thwarting your priorities without care. If you do react, some folks get annoyed or act dismissively ("C'mon, man, seriously! Quit freaking out! It's just a PIZZA!"), or they minimize ("Honey, this isn't important! Don't let it upset you!") and others just downright blow you off ("I'm done with this. When you're ready to calm down, fine. Otherwise, sulk—see if I care").

Basically, it all boils down to the fact that Aspies *and* NTs need to think less about reacting or assuming and more about reflecting and really, really listening.

Make me see what you see.

Activity 3

LEGO MY CREATION!

Ready, Set

It's a key phrase to use in improving both written and spoken communication, and it takes practice to do that. So, what better way to practice communication than with toys? And what better toy than the Asperkid favorite, Lego?

Here's what you'll need:

- two small containers, each holding an identical assortment of "parts"— Lego bricks or figures, building blocks, styrofoam balls and pipe cleaners. Anything works as long as both containers contain the same objects.

Go!

Sit your two contestants back to back, and give each one a container that has items in it which are identical to their partner's. For example, my kids chose to work with Lego: each person received a mini-figure, hair, a flower, a blue brick, a red brick, a Lego castle chain, a window pane, a Lego treasure chest and two small Lego "studs."

Player 1 had three minutes to construct whatever he wanted out of the pieces—the only rule was that he had to use them all (oh! and NO PEEKING from Player 2).

1. When time was up, he would explain to his sister what he saw in front of him (I call it, "Make me see what you see") and how she could make the same thing. She was to repeat back the instructions that she heard (which weren't always accurate, nor were they always what he'd meant to say), giving them a chance to clarify and redirect.

2. After she'd added on whatever pieces he'd described, she'd repeat back to him, "Ok, so you see a…" If that was right, they'd move on. If not, another chance to clarify, describe and correct.

3. And so they began. "Put the mini-figure on the red brick," he started. Well, this sounded pretty good, but in all honesty, it needed to be a lot more specific: was the red brick facing him with the long or short end? And where on the brick should the figure go? The back row or the front? To the left, in the middle or to the right? Hanging off an edge? And was she wearing her hair? (It'd be the same as if your spouse said, "I feel like having Chinese," so you scramble to get lo mein for dinner…when he was actually craving egg rolls! We have to be precise in order to get or produce the sought-after goal.)

4. Two things happened right away. First, Sean needed some coaching to help him to "paint" a clear "word picture" to describe what he saw. That goes to the mind blindness and also to some word retrieval/working memory challenges. No big deal.

5. The second thing, however, was that his extremely verbose sister started asking him lots of questions right away. When I asked her to hold back, she quipped, "What? I'm not allowed to communicate with my partner?" After all, she thought she was doing what had been asked of her. Of course she could ask questions, but here's the key: **communication goes two ways. When we don't allow others the time they need to think and process, we take over, wresting control, denying our teammates the chance to improve their skills and lowering their sense of accomplishment.** Before asking questions, we ALL need to LISTEN PATIENTLY. That's especially true when listening to Asperkids. Sean needed his sister to wait, I explained, until he was done giving directions. Then, if she still needed clarification, of course she could ask. Interrupting or diving in right away—even with the best of motives—doesn't feel helpful to others; it feels bossy (a very common Aspie "teamwork troublespot").

6. Ten, deeply attentive minutes later, they had done it. The Lego sculptures were perfectly identical…and the little team was so happy that they kept playing until Mom had to break up the fun for dinner.

"We rock!" I heard Sean say to his big sister. And with a big hug for her lil' bro, she agreed, "Yeah, Sean. We do!"

You can **adjust the complexity of this game by the number and size of pieces involved**. Fewer items that are larger in size are easier for young children (think Duplo blocks, cotton swabs or toothpicks), while teens can work up to as many as they'd like, getting as intricate as is challenging but still fun (circuitry, glass beads, small elastic bands, etc.).

Activity 4

GAMING: EXTRA TIPS FOR EVERYONE

Ready, Set, Go!

That zinger. That one-liner. Even that flirtatious quip. Who hasn't looked back in time and said to themselves, "Oh! I wish I could've thought in the moment!" Spontaneous communication can be tough—especially for Aspies. That's why Asperkids really benefit from scripts— pre-imagined, pre-practiced "lines" which you can help them devise, to be used as social situations demand. According to Shakespeare, "All the world's a stage." Well, Asperkids need to know their lines ahead of time. Practice reflective listening, giving positive feedback to others and building on each other's ideas rather than deciding either/or, your or mine.

There are "rules" to all group activities, but a lot of them are unspoken and implied. Asperkids need everything to be succinct and explicit. Period. Moreover, expectations have to be clearly set before trouble ensues, not afterwards. This weekend, I heard my children arguing over whether or not someone had won the board game they played. They hadn't agreed to the rules before they began, and now there was trouble. Unless we explain what "being a good girl" or "playing nicely" looks like in our minds, how can we expect children to guess? **Fair play means everyone knows what is expected— with illustrative examples of success and defined rules or boundaries—beforehand.**

Present a clear and consistent picture of what others will consider to be demonstrations of good teamwork (at home and

at school). Continue to illustrate, through your own behavior, that **showing respect for other people's opinions is not the same thing as agreeing with them**. It just means that you accept their right to believe and be who and what they want to without your judgment.

Ready for more? Good.

- Have all of your supplies and equipment ready *before* they are needed. Making others wait for you causes frustration and annoyed feelings.

- Be on time whenever your teammates need you.

- Know the rules of the game and follow them. No excuses.

- You know how good (or not-so-good) you are at an activity. Let everyone discover that without your bragging OR putting yourself down.

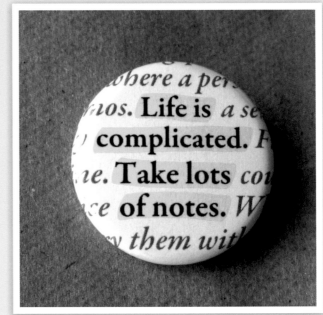

- No eye rolling, no annoyed sighs. No yelling or walking away. No quitting. Those are all ways of playing "down."

- Don't make excuses; learn from mistakes, shake them off and move on.

- Accept judgment calls even if you think they're wrong.

- Stay in control of your emotions. People respect a good loser. Even your teammates don't want to be around a sore loser.

- Be kind to EVERYONE. Whether it's a tennis match or a game of Monopoly, encourage your teammates AND your opponents—no matter what. Congratulate their effort regardless of their success.

- Leave the play space in even better shape than you found it.

Finally: About Competition and "Other" Teams

Whether competing against a sibling, a school group, a team or even just against his own perfectionist demands of himself, an Asperkid (like all kids) needs to be taught good sportsmanship. But take your time delving into the world of competitive activities; an Asperkid is already her own worst critic. Stick with cooperative games until she is able to follow rules and maintain emotional control during and at the end of a game. Follow the Asperkid's lead: if he really prefers cooperative games, stay with those. Challenge him as much as is comfortable, but always respect his personality and his developmental pace without criticism.

Snapshot-Sized Fun

WHERE DO I FIT IN?

Ready, Set

Whether teaching a young child about seconds/minutes/hours/days/weeks/months, our house/street/city/state/country/continent/hemisphere/planet/solar system/galaxy, or an older child subatomic particles/atom/element/molecule/compound, make part/to whole/to bigger-whole/to bigger-whole a concrete visual-kinetic experience; whether talking about mosaics of perspectives or members of a family or team—knowing "where I fit in" is important for everyone.

Here's what you'll need:

- nesting boxes; jewelry box to tissue box to shoebox and so on, or a collection of boxes from a craft store (these boxes double as nesting blocks and make a really cool-looking tower with lots of inherent lessons in part/whole, comparing sizes, etc.)

- markers/paint pens/paints

- Lego minifigure, small doll or similar, to represent the individual Asperkid.

Go!

1. Decorate and label the boxes to fit the subject at hand (see suggestions above).

2. Present the concept from smallest up, beginning with the individual. For example, show the figure or doll and say, "This is you, and you are part of this family. Without you, the family is incomplete." Then place the figure inside the "family" box, and close the lid. "Our family is part of this community," and so on, always reminding before the lid closes that without each precursor ("you," "our family," "this community," etc.) this particular group would not be whole.

3. Once you've reached the last box, ask, "Let's try to remember EVERYTHING that was essential to the calendar year/chemical compound/universe TOGETHER."

4. Now recite the list backwards. You might say, "The universe is made up of ALL of its galaxies, ours is the Milky Way." Remove the Milky Way galaxy box. "The Milky Way is made up of ALL of the stars it contains, we call ours the sun." And so on.

5. Practice backwards and forwards, allowing the Asperkid to stack box upon box, building and deconstructing the tower. While practicing the vocabulary, always recall: **no team, system or community is complete if any smaller part is missing.**

Chapter 3

HOW MUCH "MATTER" CAN YOU STUFF IN THERE?

Personal Priorities, Meet Your Team

. . . .

Included Activities

1. Enter Mountain Pose

2. The Tower of Density

Primary psycho-social skills
Impulsivity
Perspective-taking

Motor and processing skills
Attention
Bilateral coordination
Cognitive
Fine motor skills
Language processing
Motor planning
Problem solving
Sensory processing
Social skills (turn taking)
Visual processing
Working memory

Teaching/learning styles
Active
Auditory
Global
Intuitive
Kinesthetic
Reflective
Visual

Academic enrichment and reinforcement
Language arts (handwriting, spelling and writing)
Math
Science

The kids don't know it, but my husband grabs a handful of peanut M&M candies after every meal. He walks away from the (often chaotic) table into the laundry room, rummages in the "sweets stash," and spends about a minute munching in solitude. Now, like I said, I'm the only one who knows about his little ritual, so if "life happened" and he was suddenly prevented from sneaking away, no other "Team O'Toole" members would understand why Dad seemed irritable or unnerved. And even if everyone knew that Dad was off having a handful of candy, they probably wouldn't understand how incredibly powerful even the most "inconsequential things" can be to Aspies.

Priorities are, after all, tremendously personal. And for folks on the spectrum, who are naturally more self-referenced, it can be VERY difficult to "roll with" small changes that, to us, don't seem as logical or important as the original plan—often to the detriment of the overall experience.

Let me set a scene you'll understand well. Imagine that you've spent the entire day looking forward to something—a night out with friends, a long-overdue dinner date with your spouse, maybe a haircut (alone) or an uninterrupted shower that lasts long enough to shave both legs. Whatever the specifics, logic tells you this isn't a big "to do" in the scheme of things. Still, that "something" *feels* really important to *you*.

Now suppose dinner gets cancelled or the hot water runs out. Just like that, plans change. And at that point, all you really and truly want to do is stomp your feet, yell at everybody, slam a door and sit down for a good cry. You may not be on the spectrum, but that, friends, is a meltdown. And everyone's had them.

Are you entitled to a momentary loss of cool? Yes. You're human. And while everybody may keep it together some of the time, nobody keeps it together ALL of the time—especially when we feel "gypped," duped or unheard. But **for Asperkids, a "switcharoo" feels like an intensely personal insult**.

We Aspies cling to our rigid thinking for a reason: safety. **Inflexible routines, rituals, interests and social scripts create a feeling of order in a chaotic world.** When that small bit of control—a favorite seat, a bedtime routine or the best parking spot—is tossed aside, the Asperkid, too, feels unimportant. Meltdowns or tantrums ensue, everyone gets stressed and nobody communicates. Anything that could have been informative and loving deteriorates into chaos, frustration and tears. Not. Good.

Perception and reality are very closely related. In order to minimize EVERYONE's frustration and confusion, adults have to help bring the two together. Here's the game plan:

- A strong team has goals that are clear and commonly agreed upon (that's what we practiced establishing in the last chapter).

- In order for desired goals to be achieved, other (often less exciting but very important) foundational tasks *must* be accomplished first ("have-to-dos").

- If the goal is to be reached, no one person's personal priority can outweigh the team "have-to-dos."

Above all, teammates need each others' respect and compassion. These kids do best when given context and logic. So, **take the time to acknowledge their disappointment if a particular personal sacrifice is necessary.** Don't accept discourtesy or aggression, of course, but remember that a little compassion (which is not the same as appeasement!) goes a long way with anyone. Once the team has established its goals, how do you help an Asperkid SEE the incredibly abstract and subjective lines between personal and group priorities? I'm so glad you asked.

Here's what you'll need: nothing. Just yourself.

Activity 1

ENTER MOUNTAIN POSE

Ready, Set

My kids were messing around with their balance one afternoon. Overhearing their discussion, my mind began to wander until I stopped to wonder something: did they know what it meant if someone was described as "centered"? Sometimes it feels as if I certainly don't. Teachers are overworked and underpaid. Families are overstressed. We aren't so good at keeping people, teams or systems balanced…calm…centered. Often, it means choosing subtle over grand and "we" over "me"—a really tall order for many people, and most especially for Asperkids.

Let me give you a personal example. When I began writing this chapter, I happened to have the flu. That morning, rather than getting everyone up, dressed and fed and out the door to school on time, I would much have preferred to stay asleep. But, that wasn't an option.

So, I woke the kids, and rather pitifully asked them to please get dressed and down to breakfast without requiring a second call. I felt awful, I explained, and really needed their help. Thirty minutes later, the eldest two

were still straggling in their rooms and I was really upset. Even though I know they didn't think of their dawdling as selfish, it sure felt that way to me. In truth, though, they weren't being intentionally hurtful or disrespectful. Mentally, they'd never gotten past the "me" to the "we."

Maybe, then, this is actually a little bit of purposeful play for *all* of us. Let's all pay attention to what "balance" *really* feels like.

Experts say that the yoga pose called "Mountain Pose" (tadasana) helps improve balance and develops a sense of personal center. In all honesty, it pretty much looks like you're just standing there. But who cares? If nothing else, it's a good chance to laugh together—and best case scenario, you'll make a point: **achieving and sustaining balance has to be deliberate.**

Go!

Here's what you do:

1. Stand with your feet together and your arms at your sides. Press your weight evenly across the balls and arches of your feet. Breathe steadily. Focus on right now.

2. Press your big toes together (separate your heels if you need to). Lift your toes and spread them apart. Then, place them back down on the mat, one at a time. (If you have trouble balancing, stand with your feet six inches apart or wider.)

3. Draw down through your heels and straighten your legs. Ground your feet firmly into the earth, pressing evenly across all four corners of both feet.

4. Then, lift your ankles and the arches of your feet. Squeeze your outer shins toward each other.

5. Draw the top of your thighs up and back, engaging the quadriceps. Rotate your thighs slightly inward, widening your sit bones.

6. Tuck in your tailbone slightly, but don't round your lower back. Lift the back of your thighs, but release your buttocks. Keep your hips even with the center line of your body.

7. Bring your pelvis to its neutral position. Do not let your front hip bones point down or up; instead, point them straight forward. Draw your belly in slightly.

8. As you inhale, elongate through your torso. Exhale and release your shoulder blades away from your head, toward the back of your waist.

9. Broaden across your collarbones, keeping your shoulders in line with the sides of your body.

10. Press your shoulder blades toward the back ribs, but don't squeeze them together. Keep your arms straight, fingers extended and triceps firm. Allow your inner arms to rotate slightly outward.

11. Elongate your neck. Your ears, shoulders, hips and ankles should all be in one line.

12. Keep your breathing smooth and even. With each exhalation, feel your spine elongating. Softly gaze forward. Hold the pose for up to one minute.

Yep…like I said…you're pretty much standing there. But hold it for long enough, and you'll notice how many teeny adjustments you have to constantly make to maintain center. **Balance won't happen by accident** in yoga—or in life. It takes constant reminders and perpetual effort.

It also takes…(echo voice on!) **the Tower of Density** (density, density…).

Activity 2

THE TOWER OF DENSITY

Ready, Set
Here's what you'll need:

- dark corn syrup

- water

- vegetable oil

- liquid dish soap (ideally Dawn brand)

- honey

- lamp oil

- pure maple syrup

- tall glass cylinder (like a vase)—1 liter/1000ml capacity (alternatively, you can use multiple clear soda bottles without their labels)

- liquid food coloring

- eight identical plastic or paper cups

- kitchen scale

- a grape tomato OR a plastic bottle cap

- a single popcorn kernel

- a basic balance—you can even use a piece of wood and a triangular block for a fulcrum.

Go!

You've probably guessed by now that I may have a bit of a flare for drama. Hokey? Yes, maybe a little bit. But, as I learned while teaching both middle and high school, upping the "showmanship" ante really helps drive home important points, even to the most jaded of teenagers. So when I gathered the Asperkids around the Tower of Density (insert echo), I introduced it just that way—with a booming announcer voice and great, sweeping Las Vegas-style pomp. Folks, you only go around once. Go for it.

First, allow the Asperkid to assemble the balance, whether building it out of a block and wooden plank or assembling a simple, dime-store plastic version like I have.

Where, I asked, did the fulcrum have to be for the balance to be steady? The youngest moved it from side to side, experimenting independently until he had proven to himself that yes, the balance point had to be centered. (Hint, hint—review the term "centered"!)

The Tower is a great illustration of what really "matters" (pun intended) which can be appreciated by all ages. Technically, it's a rainbow-colored, fun-to-make, multilayered demonstration of density and specific gravity (which you may not have thought about since chemistry class). The liquids will separate into colorful bands, communicating, in a concrete way, the differing amounts of actual matter crammed into each, as well as the amount of "how much it matters" the layers symbolically contain.

To begin our experiment, Sean put his plastic cup on a scale and measured out, by weight, eight ounces of corn syrup. Then, I asked him to place it on one side of the small, plastic balance we'd set up.

I put an empty cup on the other side of the balance, and challenged his older (and a bit more dexterous) older sister to fill the other cup with just enough water (colored with bright blue food dye) so that—even without measuring its weight—we'd know we had eight ounces on each side.

This begs the question: why not just let her weigh the water on the kitchen scale? Two reasons.

First, "shaking things up" is extremely important for our Asperkids' cognitive flexibility, keeping them out of mental/emotional ruts that will otherwise leave them stranded. Obviously, at ten years old, Maura knew she could weigh eight ounces easily using the scale. But I wanted her

to extend her thinking—and she did, filling the second cup until the balance was level.

And, believe it or not, this actually led to a discussion about algebra and solving for the unknown that would "balance" the equation.

My second goal was for the Asperkids to see (not just be told) that weight and mass aren't exactly the same thing. Indeed, they quickly noticed that it took more of one liquid (like water) and less of another (like honey) to equal out the balance, which only measures weight. Their eyes, however, were perceiving the difference in "mass"—the amount of matter (stuff) crowded into something.

Without warning, I quickly corralled the team into a small bathroom, shutting the door. Like something out of a 1920s telephone booth game, we were SQUISHED. That's dense matter! Then, I opened the door and (without guidance) they began to meander out. And there was nature's love of balance—release some "molecules" (or Asperkids) and matter is less smooshed.

On and on we went, pouring and measuring—using proprioceptive input to gauge speed, viscosity, and weight…challenging bilateral coordination and fine motor control…

filling cups one-at-a-time with green dish soap, vegetable oil, pure maple syrup, corn syrup, and last, honey.

Next, we used a permanent marker to label the three cups containing vegetable oil, lamp oil and water. These would represent life's "want to dos"—experiences that supported a team's goals but weren't necessary for its survival.

In our "team," where "being safe and feeling loved" were the stated goals, "wants" included family game nights, unexpected adventures and surprises.

The remaining cups (syrup, soap and honey) held the "have-to-dos"—those tasks that were essential for the team to thrive and for our goals to be possible. The particular "wants" and "have-to-dos" will vary depending upon your own "team" goals.

For example, "Team O'Toole" came up with:

- "Doing our jobs"—for adults, that meant our careers, for kids, schoolwork and for everyone—chores to keep the house safe and healthy.

- "Following rules" was another, both for the kids who needed to trust us even when they didn't understand or agree, and for Mom and Dad, who have to follow certain community rules to be good and lawful citizens.

- "Being kind to each other." That, we agreed, included treating other team members (and their property) as we would want to be treated.

With priorities clearly listed, it was time to assemble the Tower. Here's how you can do the same:

- Pour each liquid, one at a time, into the cylinder or vase SLOWLY and WITHOUT TOUCHING THE SIDES if possible ("center" it).

- The liquids MUST go in as follows: honey, corn syrup, liquid dish soap, water, vegetable oil, lamp oil.

Even if they mix a little bit, you will (eventually) have a rainbow of distinct densities—each liquid separating itself from the others due to its own unique composition.

Notice: **the "have-to-dos" all settle at the bottom like a foundation or dense platform upon which the rest of the goals can be built. There is more "stuff that matters" packed into a smaller volume of "have-to-dos" than in any single person's "want-to-do."**

Pretty cool, huh? But there's even more. Remember the whole big set-up about looking forward to something that gets sidetracked unexpectedly? We can build that into the

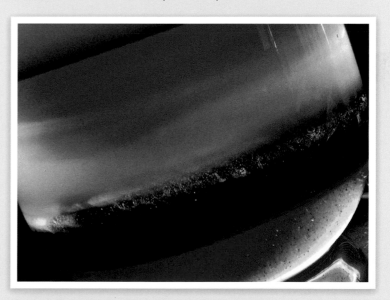

demonstration, too. Let's say each team member has hypothetically completed his or her have-to-dos…the team is running smoothly and it's time to enjoy the want-to-dos.

Now enters the (dreaded) unexpected turn-of-events…in the form of a plastic bottle cap or a grape tomato and a single popcorn kernel.

The cap or grape tomato represents a BIG special interest related "want-to-do": a new video game, Pokemon cards or the just-released sequel to a favorite book. To make the point, it must be a "want-to-do" that *feels* enormously important to the Asperkid, however uninteresting it might seem to anyone else.

BUT…lift up the single popcorn kernel. This tiny kernel represents some unexpected, important turn of events…maybe an absent friend, short funds, a rearranged school schedule or rained-out picnic. In short, it's a disappointing change in plans.

Ask: "In real life, what would it feel like to have the thing you'd counted on suddenly pushed aside?" It might hurt. It might feel scary. Every feeling we have is allowed. It's OK to be upset, disappointed, angry or frustrated when expectations are dashed. In fact, it's normal. But no matter *how* we feel, every individual is responsible for his own actions and words. Period. Be sure to teach coping skills when they are *not needed* (see "Planks in the Living Room" in Chapter 6), and insist they're used when the time comes.

From a LOW height, drop the kernel into the Tower. It will sink all the way down to the corn syrup level; that, you will recall aloud, is a "have-to-do" spot.

Now, allow an Asperkid to GENTLY drop the bottle cap (let it fill up) or the grape tomato into the center of the Tower. Either will sink, but only just slightly. Both the cap and the tomato are bigger than the kernel. And they *do* "matter" (they're not floating on top as would a ping pong ball)…but as big as they look and feel, they just don't "matter as much" as the tiny, dense corn kernel. Why?

Facts don't change because of feelings. No matter how much a "want-to-do" FEELS like a "have-to-do," it just isn't.

Reassure younger "teammates" that you, too, get mad, sad and utterly peeved when you feel let down. That's not the end of the story, though. By taking these steps, a team can move past obstacles, getting back on course toward the "want-to-dos":

- Express feelings using "I feel" statements (without blaming a person or preventing the "have-to-do" from happening).

- Pitch in, if needed—with a GOOD attitude (it's a "have-to-do," it has "more matter," so it HAS to happen first).

- Don't lose sight of the goal! *Prove* that "have-to-dos" don't obliterate "wants."

- Move on, congratulate the team and get back on track towards that well-earned "bottle cap" as soon as you possibly can.

Chapter 4

THE FOREST, THE TREES AND THE SUM OF THE PARTS

. . . .

Included Activities

1. Bug's Eye View

2. Find That Analogy!

3. The "Pointillism" of Art

4. Supersize It!

   Snapshot-Sized Fun: Glowing Water

Primary psycho-social skills
Inclusion
Part-to-whole relationships
Perception versus fact

Motor and processing skills
Attention
Auditory motor integration
Bilateral coordination
Cognitive
Fine motor skills
Language processing
Motor planning
Problem solving
Sensory processing
Sequencing
Social skills (turn taking)
Visual motor integration
Visual processing
Visualization
Visual-verbal
Working memory

Teaching/learning styles
Active
Auditory
Global
Intuitive
Kinesthetic
Reflective
Sensing
Visual

Academic enrichment and reinforcement
Language arts (spelling, speaking and listening, writing)
Math
Science
Social studies

Gestalt. It's a strange-sounding psychological term that basically means "the big picture," the "whole enchilada," the entirety of a situation. It's the forest in "not seeing the forest for the trees." And often, our kiddos are the ones missing it.

Part of diagnosing Asperger's or autism actually requires a noted fascination with "parts" of things, rather than with the "whole thing." It's just the way we think. For example, some Asperkids (generally boys) find the symbiotic relationship between wheel and axis utterly fascinating. An Aspergirl might be entranced with words—not conversation, but etymology, grammatical functions, word puzzles and poetic rhythms. It's that characteristic preference for parts that makes for lovers of Lego, complex jigsaw puzzles, family trees and cataloged collections.

Make no mistake: there is value in our way of seeing the world. I took this photo in the British Museum, where the play of dappled late afternoon sunlight on the ancient tiles was simply beguiling.

There were veins of black amidst the ambers, each selected by some long ago hand to complement its neighbor. I could almost sense that artist, twisting the stones this way or that until they suited him.

Then—at just the right angle—he would lay them so that their individual beauty was enhanced and set off the adjacent pieces. What unimaginable patience and vision this artist had, I remember thinking. What sheer determination and total absorption in the tiny bits in his finger tips.

Here's the catch: I was the only person standing a breath away from the tiles. The other onlookers were feet behind me—looking at the entire gorgeous mosaic.

Eventually, I, too, stepped back to take in the "gestalt" of the work. But even now, what I most recall was that craftsman's ability to appreciate the subtleties of even the smallest pieces as he built them into a grander whole.

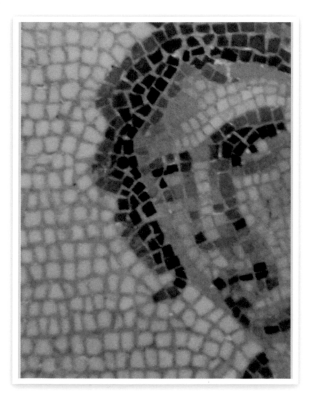

Sometimes, I'll be honest, I feel sorry for NTs. They really don't appreciate the microcosmic patterns, connections and rhythms are necessary to construct bigger ideas. Aspies see beauty there—in hypnotic order, astounding simplicity and inherent complexities.

And so, I don't believe one perspective, Aspie or NT, is better than the other. It's like looking at the mosaic. Up close (à la Aspie), the tiny tiles are beautiful in themselves. That said, I can see the trouble getting lost in pieces and missing the "bigger picture"— which I jokingly call "getting right to the toenail of the matter."

At some point, I learned to try to take a step back and see the larger view (something that's still unnatural and challenging). For many reasons, all Asperkids need to learn the same skill. A complete perspective, after all, is inclusive; individual points of view are part of a larger whole.

Consider how very many small, mundane bits of life add up to the big, important moments. For example: if a teacher gives a summary of what will be on the final, and the Asperkid merely writes down that there will be a final, he's going to have a problem. Maybe a friend is upset and sharing an avalanche of thoughts. Can the well-meaning Asperkid understand what's bothering her friend and respond accordingly? Relationships require the personal restraint and maturity to acknowledge that one's own perception isn't the final say on what is or isn't so. Life (and everyone in it) expects us to stop, check and reconsider.

A Bit of Biology

The challenge of being able to grasp the "whole" from its "parts" goes beyond the psychological. In fact, it's is actually mirrored by a specific visual perception skill called "visual closure." Basically, that's the ability to correctly generalize a whole picture by seeing a part of it—much as one could (or could not) generalize a fact or rule to a universal application (i.e. "Don't cross the street" means ALL streets, not just this one). Perhaps not so surprisingly, many Aspies' visual closure skills, like our generalization skills, are markedly weak.

Why might this matter? It turns out that the ability to visualize a complete whole from incomplete information directly affects reading fluency and speed, recognizing sight words, making inferences, predicting outcomes, completing one's own thoughts and making accurate deductions (as in mathematics, science, and reading comprehension). Asperkids who are particularly challenged in visual closure may mix up words with close beginning or endings, struggle with project (or time) planning, spelling patterns, coloring, analogies, word finds or visualizing and completing entire processes (both academic and practical).

Now here's the cool part: as we help kids strengthen their visual closure skills, their understanding of part-to-whole relationships seems to improve, too. In other words, this is really important stuff. We see in part. We know in part. And we have to integrate EVERY part to see the "whole truth." How? Let's begin by being bugs.

Activity 1

BUG'S EYE VIEW

Ready, Set
Here's what you'll need:

- a smartphone or tablet with built-in camera or just an instant camera

- a defined area (like your backyard, a park, your classroom, your home, etc.).

Bug's Eye View is a scavenger hunt (which by definition is already fun) in which the trick of succeeding is to be able to assume the physical perspective of a bug. It's a foundational platform upon which any number of extensions into the idea of "perspective" can be built.

In my experience, kids of all ages—which means adults, too—love scavenger hunts. You get to run around, burn energy and be a little bit frantic all at once. So, this game will work for preschoolers as well as it will for teens; just amp up the challenges as skills dictate.

Remember, too, that in any group, one personality (or maybe simply the eldest) will naturally dominate. That's alright sometimes, but not all the time. Insist either that the youngest or least vocal be in charge during some rounds, or simply separate the group into pairs, ensuring that no one "falls through the cracks" or is marginalized.

That being said, Bug's Eye View involves two jobs:

1. Photo Taker: at first, this is the adult in charge or eldest players

2. Object Finder: at first, the youngest or least confident players.

Go!

Round 1: First, the Photo Taker is armed with the camera, tablet or phone and allowed to roam around the designated play area snapping pictures (without being watched!). Remember the name of the game: Bug's Eye View. If you were a bug, everything in the yard, class or house would seem enormous—on a completely different scale than we see it as humans.

In order to capture that perspective in a photo, the camera has to zoom in really, really close. This means, of course, that mundane, familiar objects are going to look totally foreign.

In other words: a change in point of view means a change in what and how the world is observed.

When we played the game, I took the first photos to demonstrate what to do. First, I snapped the criss-crossing ropes in our backyard hammock.

Next was the green plastic of the swing. I was purposely starting off easy.

There were no other white, woven ropes or green plastic in the play area—so intrinsically, I was setting my players up to succeed.

Then, I handed the camera to my middle son who LOVED the idea of being in control of the camera. He got very close to the lettering on the trash can, the netting on the trampoline, a particular flower…getting trickier and tricker as he went (for example, there was more than one pink rose bush—so which was the one in the photo?). Eventually, there were about ten "bug's eye view" locations that had been photographed. And, to encourage the Object Finders as they went, we left a little golden star sticker at each location.

It was time to get the Object Finders! We began with a brief (and silly) reminder—but important enough to the overall lesson that I would repeat it (changing style not substance) for any age. Gavin, my preschooler, and his "betrothed" sat with me, each holding a small magnifying glass. "Now, let me ask you one quick question before you get going: if you were little, tiny bugs…would I look the same to you as I do now?" They thought about this. Of course, I'd still be me, they agreed. I'd still be a girl. And I'd still have red hair.

"True! But what about my size?" I asked, and they agreed, in the end, that to a bug I'd probably look big, "Like a giant." At my encouragement, they held up their magnifying glasses, drawing in very close. "You look silly!" they said. Silly and really, really different. Could they see my whole body any more? Or even my whole face? Nope.

The closer we are to something, the less we can see of the whole picture. (How very true in so many ways.)

That, I explained, was called "point of view" or "perspective." **Depending upon how we experience the world, our "perspectives" can change a whole lot.** Now, they were going to hunt around the yard, using their magnifying glasses and my phone (squeals!) to identify the "whole object" that had previously been photographed from a "bug's eye view."

They'd be matching part-to-whole and would be asked to explain their conclusions along the way.

Giggles of delight rang out (as did a few minor arguments until I helped them take turns holding the phone)—and they did it, successfully finding all ten spots around the yard. (Happy dance! Happy dance!)

Round 2: When all of the objects have been found, the tides turn and the successful Object Finders become the Photo Takers. Roles reverse, "power" changes hands and with each round, you'll find the game gets trickier and trickier (and more and more fun).

Sometimes the players are going to need some clues, some encouragement to communicate more clearly and to problem-solve. "Yes," you might encourage a stumped Object Finder, "the letters are white—but is the background in the photo red like it is on this ball? No? OK, then where else could you look?" In the same way, **Asperkids will need reminders that what they see, hear and feel in the "real" world is like the "bug's eye view"—real, but only part of the bigger picture.**

Activity 2

FIND THAT ANALOGY!

Ready, Set
Here's what you'll need:

- four bags of increasing size (e.g. snack bag, sandwich bag, paper lunch bag, grocery sack)—or nesting boxes as in Chapter 2

- marker

- a chapter from a book the Asperkid has not read

- collection basket

- two index cards

- a camera/smartphone.

Until I began writing professionally, I never noticed that I use a whole lot of analogies when I teach and speak. It's not a conscious choice; it's just the best way I've found to communicate new ideas to any audience, whether high school students, preschoolers or esteemed professionals. By referring to some kind of relationship with which we are both already familiar, I can then quickly build upon it, enabling you, the reader (or listener) to easily understand unfamiliar concepts. The fancy phrase teachers use to describe this technique is "activation of prior knowledge." Personally, I just think that speaking to an audience with respect for what you already know is good manners and collegial. Oh, yes. And it works really well in making utterly foreign ideas completely approachable.

In essence, every single one of the activities in this book is an analogy, tying sensorial experiences to abstract (and often difficult) notions. That's good for a myriad of reasons,

not the least of which is that by learning to work through analogies well, we actually stretch and strengthen our Asperkids' critical thinking skills. In order to answer an analogy question correctly, the kids have to make deductions—they have to form logical relationships or "bridge" between two words. They must think about how the words are related. And, as we've already seen, that's pretty tough for a lot of Asperkids.

You may have noticed that Asperkids ask a LOT of questions about meanings, parsing terms and definitions, often of words they should understand. These kids aren't trying to be argumentative or difficult (though it may feel that way); they—we—don't mean to split hairs. No, what we are doing is trying to *precisely* understand what is being said and meant at a particular moment in time and in a particular context.

Words do, happily, represent specific items or ideas (not universals), but they can be littered with nuances and related in an infinite number of ways. That's why analogies are such a great tool for our Asperkids. Through what can (and should) feel like games, Asperkids can practice identifying and narrowing possible connections between ideas, eventually learning to focus on the most essential aspects of what is being said.

In this second scavenger hunt, we're going to very literally find the right parallels. We're going on an analogy hunt!

Go!

Before you begin, label each of the bags or boxes from smallest to largest with your home town, state, nation, continent (or go with Earth, rocky planets, solar system,

Milky Way or electron, nucleus, atom, molecule or differentiated tissues, organ, organ system, animal…or any other similar progression). Then, place the town bag inside the state, which goes inside the nation, which goes, finally, inside the continent.

Next, label the first index card WHOLE, and write this "bridge" sentence:

"A _____ is a part of _____." Then, write the following list:

- magazine

- house

- mammal

- plant

- reference book

- street

- map

- flower

- apple

- face.

On the second index card, write the title, "PARTS," and add the same bridge sentence:

"A _____ is a part of _____." Then, write the following list:

- yolk

- finger

- fur/feather

- flour

- page

- leaf

- bread slice

- buckle

- steering wheel

- word.

1. To begin, pull out the book (preferably, it's a favorite of yours that you can share later!), turn to a chapter somewhere in the middle, and begin to read aloud. Do it with gusto—give it your all…and then, after a page or two, ask for a full plot summary. Expect a perplexed look. How, you'll be asked, can anyone give you a "book report" if he's only heard a few pages without any introduction or explanation?

   Of course, you'll agree, he can't.

   Usually, ideas are related in one of several main ways: function, degree, lack, characteristic, type/kind, part-to-whole and definition, and by using a "bridge sentence" you can easily figure out the connection. For this game, we're only concerned with part-to-whole, so we need only one bridge: "A _____ is part of a _____."

2. Show the "continent" (or Earth or molecule) bag/box. For example, you say, this bag represents a "whole," and within that whole are smaller parts. Slowly, deliberately, draw out each subsequent bag.

See? The "bridge sentence" works. A city is part of a state. A state is part of a nation. In each case, the relationship is consistent: part-to-whole. Without the few pages you read, the book was incomplete. But without the other chapters, those few pages didn't get you very far. In life and in this game, every perspective has to be included to get the full story.

3. Give the Asperkid the camera, basket and the first card, explaining that the item listed is the WHOLE. Therefore, the task is to **find and either bring back or take a photo of a part of that whole** (e.g. an article from a magazine, the front door of a house).

4. Now, the game gets changed! List Two contains PARTS. Using the same bridge sentence, ask him to **photograph or collect a whole of which these items are each a part** (e.g. "A bread slice is part of a sandwich," "A buckle is part of a shoe or belt").

Ask your kiddo to come up with a few more examples of each for you to find!

For older players

1. Write more part-to-whole analogies on slips of paper, advancing the vocabulary as far as possible.

2. Cut each word pair into two parts, marking the reverse of each match with the same small shape, number or letter. This enables self-check of the work… For example, "grenadier: army" would be snipped into two pieces, with "*" written lightly on the reverse side of each. In this way, as the Asperkid tries to match part-to-whole, she has the opportunity to correct her own work or even determine answers by process of elimination, as needed.

3. Toss all the scraps into a bowl or bag and mix them around.

4. Ask the Asperkid to dump them all out and start making matches! By the way—if you decide to leave the self-check marks off, you can lay the mixed-up slips face down and make a concentration (memory) game for solo or group play.

5. Remind the Asperkid to use the bridge sentence strategy (in the game and in life)! Here are a few pairs to get you started:

"A _____ is a part of [the/a] _____."

Part	Whole
Count	Nobility
Level	Hierarchy
Installment	Serial
Rebuttal	Debate
Exosphere	Atmosphere
Thorax	Insect
Spinal cord	Vertebrate
Sect	Religion
Appetizer	Meal
Scene	Play
Vertex	Angle
Stanza	Poem

Activity 3

THE "POINTILLISM" OF ART

Ready, Set
Here's what you'll need:

- white paper

- dowels

- pencil

- watercolor or poster paint (or oil paints if you have them!) in red, blue and yellow

- ink pad—any colors

- fine-tipped paint brushes

- some or all of these: cotton swabs, lollipop sticks or new pencils (the eraser end has to be flat).

We can only see part of what there is to see; we only know part of what there is to know. That's the lesson of Bug's Eye View—and it's an ideal that you can explore on an artistic level, too.

One of the world's most famous (and fun) ways to experience the connectedness of part and whole is through pointillism, the style of art invented largely by Georges Seurat (whom my daughter calls "Seurat the Dot"—and you'll see why). The unique thing about pointillism is the way in which the paint is applied to the canvas. Thousands of tiny paint dots—each in a "pure," unmixed color—are dabbed onto the surface in such dense patterns that the art really is more about science than about its subject!

The method operates much as modern computer printers shoot out super-small dots of ink in cyan, magenta and yellow or a monitor displays pictures in what are actually tiny pixels. Essentially, pointillism takes advantage of the human eye's tendency to blur densely packed pieces—ultra-fine dots placed very closely to one another seem, to us, to be one expertly blended crystal clear image. And while we *think* we see lush greens, robust oranges and vibrant purples, we are actually perceiving the light reflected by closely placed primary colors. Make no mistake—this extension can be as simple or as complex as you want. Seurat's most famous painting, *A Sunday Afternoon in the Park*, took over two years to complete and contains about 3,456,000 dots!

Ready to explore your artistic side? Even for Asperkids who don't think they "can draw"—pointillism is very, very doable. It's a fantastic, concrete way to experience a challenging, abstract concept…and it can be awfully fun for you, too, if you paint along.

First, restate: **A complete perspective is inclusive; individual points of view are part of a larger whole.**

Print out a zoomed-in image of one of Seurat's paintings (see Resources), or find it in any *Art for Kids* book. In our experiment, the project was diffused across very different ages and abilities—so while the concept was continually reinforced, each iteration looked unique.

We began with a playlist of big band and symphonic music playing in the background (there's a reason!), and as the horns and drums jammed, the kids and I discussed what we saw in the magnified snapshot of *The Circus*: *thousands* of little, tiny dots.

Each pinpoint, I said, was sort of like an individual. It had its own identity. Its own place. Its own perspective.

Then, I showed them a print of the whole picture. Wow! They were blown away by what had become of all those dots. It was, I said, like reading a complete story—or hearing an entire song. In the music they were hearing, each instrument played its part—each voice an essential (but incomplete) part of the composite piece. In the painting, each dot had a purpose, yet didn't communicate the entire scene. In life, too, that's perspective. Each person's experiences are real. Each person's existence is intentional. But the "bigger picture" can only be appreciated by taking in the whole.

Enough observation. It's time to DO.

Go!

1. Start simple: using cotton swabs, lollipop sticks or paintbrushes, let the kids begin their pointillism experience by painting their own names in dots (remember: special interests and fun are the key to everything! Maura, the mythology-lover, wrote her name in Greek!). Depending upon age and dexterity, you may even write out the letters for the child, allowing him

to cover your handwriting in dots. Gavin, for example, used Bingo-stampers to make his dots at first, as they cover more area at a time. However, he did move on to the smaller tools, too.

2. Our next step was to make a color wheel (and Gavin had out his favorite puzzle—a wooden "flower" of primary, secondary and tertiary color blending), making yellow-orange here and red-orange there, but never actually mixing the paints. Tightly bunched, the dots seemed to blend as our eyes blurred them into new hues. Yet the dots, like people, actually remained distinct. It was similar to the way individual people's perspectives may also join into something new when they work closely together.

3. We pulled out the colored stamp pads and eraser tipped-pencils next, making "confetti" all along a strip of paper that could be (and was!) stapled to dowels and turned into streamers.

4. Then, we each chose a still-life subject that was close to our hearts: the subject can be an ancient goddess, a superhero logo, part of an historic building…anything goes. It's the kids' work, so it has to be engaging. Your only guideline is that the subject should be a singular subject—for example, a particular part of a single ancient statue rather than a busy scene in downtown Athens; a single dancer rather than a whole Degas ballet class.

5. Once you've chosen the subject, you need to get its outline on the white paper—which is easily achievable in one of several ways:

   - Your artist can sketch the outline of the subject.

   - Use large stencils or rubbing plates (see Resources).

   - You can find a "line drawing" online (type that into the search engine with the subject word).

   - You can even print a famous painting from online (see Supercoloring in Resources).

6. And you're set! Using the paintbrushes or the ends of the cotton swabs, start "dotting" in the painting of your dreams!

Activity 4

SUPERSIZE IT!

Ready, Set
Here's what you'll need:

- a prism (optional)

- chalk or pencil and crayons

- paper

- masking tape

- an image you'd like to "supersize."

Go!
Once you've explored pointillism thoroughly, it's time for the Grand Finale. With kids, that means go big or go home. So go big. It's time to create your own mural.

1. Choose an image (a map, a photo or a famous painting) that will interest the Asperkids involved.

2. Enlarge the image as much as possible, then print it out.

3. Use a permanent marker and ruler to draw gridlines across the image. If you'd like to use the driveway as your canvas, use chalk and a level to draw the same grid outside. If you're staying inside, you'll need one sheet of paper for each section of the grid (paper should be rectangular or cut into squares, depending upon how your grid is divided).

4. CHALK MURAL: Assign each section of the grid to an individual artist (if possible), using the grid to guide you as you sketch and color in one square at a time on the ground, matching the budding mural to the small original.

Look back at the grid before starting a new square to. be sure the Asperkids are referring to the correctly corresponding spot in the model. Be patient and go slowly…the goal is participation, not perfection.

5. PAPER MURAL: Give a sheet of paper to each artist and *cut up the original picture* along your marker lines. Distribute the snipped bits, then, depending upon their age, abilities and confidence, outline and color in one large paper for every piece of the model. When they are all done, take the sheets of paper and assemble them like a giant jigsaw puzzle. A little masking tape on the reverse sides will give you one, large, cohesive mural.

6. If you'd like, there are also wonderful printable PDFs of murals online (usually for sale). Just print out the pre-drawn outlines, color with pastels, paints, crayons or whatever you like and tape them all together.

You can also try cracking open a beam of sunlight with a prism. What looks like a literal white wash is, we now know, in fact, a rich rainbow of every imaginable hue. Fracture the white light into its parts, and you can clearly recognize the individual players: indigo and red, violet and yellow. They are each vibrant and beautiful. But each color is really a splinter of the larger whole—the light that warms our planet, sustains our food chain and makes Sunday afternoons ten times sweeter. Photos, analogy, pixels, prisms and grids…when we each "do our part" and take the time to consider each others' perspectives, life does, indeed, reveal a brighter, richer and grander "big picture" for us all.

Snapshot-Sized Fun

GLOWING WATER

Ready, Set

Usually, heat and light go hand-in-hand. But just because something is usually true doesn't mean it's the *only* truth (remember to consider alternative possibilities!). All you have to do is "crack" an ordinary play light stick to experience "cool light." When certain chemicals combine—as in a firefly's tail, a deep-sea fish's angler or even in a basic highlighter pen—they create "cool light," or "luminescence."

And in just a few steps, the same chemical phenomenon will turn basic tap water into bucket loads of fluorescent fun.

Here's all you'll need:

- water

- a container

- non-toxic fluorescent paint (from any craft store)

- blacklight bulb (any Walmart, craft or home improvement store).

Go!

1. Add a few tablespoons of fluorescent paint in any color into very warm or hot water.

2. Stir until completely mixed into the water.

3. Add as much water as you'd like to increase the volume, stopping before the glow is too diluted.

You've got a base for **glow-in-the-dark bubbles, slime, sensory bin water beads or rice, sensory travel bags, water balloons**…the list is endless.
    And that's IT! Now, get glowing!

Chapter 5

ILLUSIONS, SPY GAMES AND TRIANGLES

The (Continued) Possibility of More than One Truth

. . . .

Included Activities

1. Gotcha!

2. Vanishing Points

3. Drawing Hands

4. Spy Games

5. Plastic Ice Cream Trucks

6. Constructive Triangles

7. Cast a (Paper) Net

    Snapshot-Sized Fun: Cosmic Cleanup

Primary psycho-social skills

Emotional resilience
Acceptance of multiple
perspectives/opinions
Understanding difference
between perception and fact

Motor and processing skills

Attention
Auditory processing
Bilateral coordination
Cognitive
Fine motor skills
Language processing
Motor planning
Oculomotor
Problem solving
Sensory processing
Sequencing
Social skills (turn taking)
Visual motor integration
Visual processing
Visualization
Visual-verbal
Working memory

Teaching/learning styles

Active
Auditory
Global
Intuitive
Kinesthetic
Reflective
Sensing
Visual

Academic enrichment and reinforcement

Language arts (reading and handwriting)
Math
Science
Social studies

When designing the logo for my company, Asperkids LLC, I had a point to make. So many families tell me that they have never heard a single positive thing said about their children, about living life on the spectrum… about the future and its possibilities. I happen to think that's tragic. As I've said before (and probably will be repeating until I go gray), Asperger's, and for that matter, pretty much EVERYTHING in life, is a lot like having red hair.

My red hair has always been my most obvious and memorable physical feature. If you ask a new acquaintance to describe me, inevitably, the answer begins with, "Well, she has red hair…" It's what sticks in people's minds and makes me, whether I like it or not, stand out from the crowd. For many reasons, that "memorable" factor has been a "pro" in my life.

On the other hand, gingers have our built-in weaknesses. I can get a sunburn through a closed window (like a vampire, as a young Aspergirl pointed out during a recent talk!), and am allergic to pretty much every single hypoallergenic lotion, sunscreen and make-up known to mankind.

There's a flip side to everything in life—a pro to every con and a con to every pro. So how will you live your life? How will you teach an Asperkid to live hers? The American president Abraham Lincoln famously said, "You can grieve that a rosebush has thorns or celebrate that a thornbush has roses." Whether we see our lives as a succession of trials or of blessings depends, I believe, entirely on our chosen perspective.

Life is, I believe, all about chosen perspective. Hence, the logo challenge. How could one graphic convey the awesome power of the thousands of small choices we make every day? Perhaps not surprisingly, the solution was found in a scientific experiment…on perspective.

In 1915, psychologist Edgar Rubin first illustrated a particular type of optical illusion—you've seen them plenty of times for certain; it's here, in the Asperkids logo.

When Rubin created the drawing of a vase—or of two faces in profile, depending upon your perspective—he made history. Rubin was able to prove that the observer initially sees only one image, realizing the alternate, equally legitimate interpretation after time has passed or, more often, after someone else prompted a change in perspective. But try to simultaneously see both the faces AND the vase, and one interpretation would suddenly be lost.

It turns out that a single viewpoint will always occlude the other because the human mind can't operate on conflicting understandings at once. What the mind saw depended upon which perspective the observer selected. It's either faces or vase, but not both at once. Lots of folks think they can see both at once—that's an illusion. The mind *has* to switch back and forth—perhaps very rapidly, but it *has* to switch.

How we see Asperkids and how we teach them to see themselves is quite a lot like Rubin's experiment.

Asperkids live in a world of "obstacle illusions," as do we adults who support them. Like the subjects viewing Rubin's drawing, we choose our focus. Are our kids and the way they think, act, learn and feel deficient or different? Are they distinctive or defective? They cannot be both at once.

In the movie about her life, my mentor, Dr. Temple Grandin, famously intuited the tricks in perspective that could make a giant appear to become a dwarf or a ball roll uphill. Real life, too, creates distortions. Heartaches may lead us to see malintent where it is not present. Overprotection may cause us to perceive kindness where danger lurks. In other words: the way we perceive everything—literally and emotionally—is affected.

Therefore, every parent, psychologist, therapist and teacher who knows an Asperkid must choose a perspective of possibility and operate from it. "Obstacles" may necessitate detours, but they don't have to be roadblocks.

For families or teachers who find themselves constantly having to advocate for easily misunderstood kids (of all ages), life is, admittedly, more challenging, more wearing, more expensive, less private and, sadly, can feel like an endless course of having to defend yourself and your child. I know. I live it, too. And I'd be doing you a disservice (and lying myself silly) to say anything different. How do I know? Because I've also been the Asperkid. I know what it is to unwittingly contribute to the social isolation that haunts you, to sabotage yourself with perfectionism and to have no one believe that you are anything but "hypersensitive" and "too smart for your own good." And of course, this is all happening to a person who does not have a lifetime of perspective or coping skills, who hasn't lived long enough to believe that high school *isn't* the pinnacle of life or that his first love won't be the only one to ever come along.

Caring about an Asperkid means you respect him enough to bear his discomforts without protest or correction. His feelings—which will ALWAYS be different from yours—are the reality to which you must respond.

The truth is tough, but it's the truth. Life with, and for, Asperkids will not be what you expected. But it can be very good. It just depends upon the perspective you choose. That said: it's up to you, in day-to-day life, to show compassion yet maintain (and teach) a longer-term view. Any day may have been a bad day—but it is *not* a bad life. And as we all tell our children: look both ways. Always look both ways. There is something beautiful and worth being deeply grateful for in even the darkest of life's moments. Whether and how well you teach this lesson may, in fact, be the difference between whether an Asperkid grows into a resilient, determined adult or a depressed, embittered "victim."

Simultaneous Truths

If "the truth" can only be one person's version or experience, and if you argue your perception as fact until the other side gives in or gives up, has truth prevailed?

Nope. Your "truth" won via endurance, not kindness or justice. Hurt feelings won't respond to your facts. And you can't grow without considering different perspectives. When one person's "truth" overpowers another's, everyone loses.

Alright then. Is there, in fact, one "truth" that will apply to everyone? Yes. And here it is: how we respond to a mistake is far more important than having made one. Or two. Or many. Or even whether you agree we've made a mistake at all. That's true for Asperkids. It's also true for you.

Folks on the spectrum see things differently. I mean that figuratively, as in we perceive and interpret intention, body language and cause and effect differently. I also mean it literally. Physically. We miss cues you don't and we catch glimpses you miss. For instance, in order for their sleight-of-hand tricks to work, magicians rely upon an experience called "joint attention"—they expect audiences to look where the showmen look. But those of us on the spectrum don't have the same "joint attention" as NTs—we often do *not* focus where others do; so while you may follow the magician's gaze, we may just as likely be looking at his hands, clearly seeing exactly that which we're not supposed to.

Whether life seems to be a magic show or a drama, a comedy or a tragedy, we all get caught up in our own plot lines. But too often, we begin to think that we, in fact, *are* our stories. And without our realizing it, those stories begin to take on a life of their own, so that we suddenly find ourselves passive players in lives we neither want nor like. A few adults have told me that having Asperger's ruined their lives and dashed their dreams. Respectfully, I entirely and wholeheartedly disagree.

Though I didn't have a word to describe it until adulthood, I was born an Aspie. I was also born female. Could being born female be responsible for a terrible life? No. Others' misogyny or maltreatment might make a life terrible, not being female. Who we are and how we are is neither good nor bad. It just is.

Yes, others' ignorance may hurt us. Fine. When the world is dark, will we shine more determinedly or blame the shadows?

It is our daily choice to either open others' minds and hearts or to turn inward toward self-pity and bitterness. My husband, a police officer, hears similar stories in the most destitute neighborhoods. One resident will complain of systematic victimization with a disinterested sense of entitlement. Meanwhile, next door, someone in far worse steads sees a life full of small blessings and a benevolent plan much greater than their own. There is a saying that goes, "The surest way to make God laugh is to tell Him your plans." We usually don't end up where we expect we will. Life is full of curveballs and completely without guarantees. So what? We may see, if we are humble enough to accept the possibility, that wherever we end up is far more amazing than we ever could have dreamed for ourselves.

I am an Aspie. And my life is wonderful, thank you very much. It is not perfect. It is not always easy. But it is extraordinary and surprising because I am not so arrogant as to think I always know what IS. I have learned that, strange as it may seem, more than one truth exists simultaneously, and that it is always within my power to say— at any point—no, this is not how the story ends. I will shine..and I will hold a light aloft for you.

But first…I'm going to trick you (with some optical illusions, that is!).

Activity 1

GOTCHA!

Ready, Set
Here's what you'll need:

- a ruler or straight-edge

- a pencil.

The concept being taught through this game is that more than one thing can be true at once…that we may perceive a situation (or idea) differently than another person does, and BOTH may be so. Or, "distortions" in the way we perceive (or don't perceive) the world may create misperceptions of what actually is.

Most Asperkids have probably seen optical illusions before, but may not know how or why they work. So, begin with a quick explanation. Optical (meaning "having to do with the eye") illusions (from the Latin for "trick") use color, light and patterns to create images that can fool our brains into seeing (or not seeing) what is actually in front of us.

When we look at something, the information gathered by the eye is sent to the brain for "processing" or figuring out. Imagine your brain as a tiny, ever-alert judge inside your head, constantly making decisions about the "evidence" gathered by whatever you may see, feel, taste, hear or smell. Usually, our brains are pretty good at matching perception to reality. But not always. But, in special circumstances, the information that reaches our brains is misleading, creating a perception that in reality, does not match what we are actually seeing. And that, you should point out, is sort of like people. Sometimes we think we KNOW for sure what is happening around us, when, in fact, we've got it quite mixed-up. That's why we have to learn to respond to others' feelings…not to our own perception of the facts.

Go!

Show the following images and questions:

Take another look at the Asperkids logo.

What do you see?

Two faces? A candlestick (or vase or chess piece)?

Which line is longer?

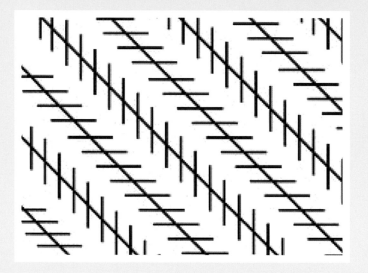

Do the lines look parallel? Turn the page so that you're looking at the lower left corner. Now do they seem to be parallel?

What's going on? Simple. Your eyes are playing tricks on you.

- Asperkids logo: The brain identifies an object by noticing its edges—separating it from its background. Whichever part of the picture you choose to "see" as the background determines that the other image is "dominant." That's the one you will "see."

- Lines: This is "the Muller-Lyer illusion." The lines themselves are exactly the same length (have the Asperkid measure them with the ruler), but the "fins" are what throw us off. The exact reason behind the confusion has been debated. However, the general thought is that the angles created by the "tails" trigger our brains' depth perception pathways, causing the "closed" arrows to appear shorter than the open center line. Oddly enough, this illusion is much more powerful in people who live in urban or suburban environments and are surrounded by the straight edges of buildings more frequently.

- The diagonal lines *are* all parallel. However, because of the hash marks shooting off in every which way, our brains' sense of orientation in space gets confused. As a result, we see the lines converging and diverging, when in fact they are perfectly straight. M.C. Escher, the graphic artist famous for his explorations of infinity and "unreachable realities," took advantage of quirks in perspective. Quite naturally, Escher's art—truthfully, all art—lends itself to an exploration of point of view, both in a visual and psychological sense. Great literature can achieve the same, as sweeping fantasies and historical adventures can tempt us into a world of characters, circumstances, reactions and influences that are completely foreign. This is a particularly important exercise for Asperkids. Those of us on the spectrum must learn and constantly remember to acknowledge the validity of others' world-views. Stepping outside of our own perceptions is completely counterintuitive.

Activity 2

VANISHING POINTS

Ready, Set

Here's what you'll need:

- stencils or objects to trace some basic shapes

- pencil

- drawing paper

- crayons, colored pencils or pastels.

Go!

Psychologists call the inborn ability to intuit other people's perspectives "theory of mind." Everyone else calls it "standing in someone else's shoes." We Aspies can't—not won't, can't—do it naturally (at least not well). We aren't self-centered. We literally cannot anticipate another's feelings without having to think through—to intellectualize—them. Compassion we have in utter droves. Natural empathy, however, largely eludes us. In order to understand what is *actually* happening in any social situation—you have to be able to see the world from someone else's perspective. And for many Aspies, that's terrifying. Why? Well, try to take a step into *our* shoes.

We are expected to perceive one set of circumstances yet react to perspective or "reality" that is invisible to us. We literally have to unlearn the natural ways we see, hear and understand the world and, instead, assume that our "take" on things is most likely skewed. And we have to do it calmly. All the time. In school. At work. In our marriages. All the time.

My (Aspie) husband described the experience like seeing something sunshiny, buttercup yellow—and everyone else swears it's green. I'd take it a step further. First, we have to remember to stop whatever we are doing or feeling long enough (and soon enough) to hear you say that the color isn't yellow…it may contain yellow (we may have gotten some of the right message), but others see green. And, no matter how certain we are in what we see or feel or hear, we have to—at least to some degree—believe you.

Aspies of *all* ages need constant and compassionate reminders to:

- STOP the forward momentum of emotions or reaction

- ASK FOR AND LISTEN TO others' perspectives

- RECONSIDER what we *know* to be true.

This, I hope you can appreciate, is really, really hard. Which is why we adults have to consciously and creatively teach our Asperkids to think globally and more three-dimensionally. And exploring perspective through art is a great way to start.

1. Ask the Asperkid to trace the shapes around the page—we had a square, triangle, oval, circle and rectangle. Then color the shapes brightly.

2. Next, make a single dot anywhere on the page. This is called our "vanishing point."

3. Using the ruler, invite the Asperkid to draw straight lines connecting that point to every corner of every shape. These lines show depth—as if we could fall into the page to another place where we, simply put, are not.

4. Repeat this for all of the shapes. For curvilinear shapes, just draw two lines, one to either side.

5. Try experimenting with the colors and different amounts of pressure (darker toward the vanishing point) to achieve subtle shading, which increases the sense of perspective.

6. Try the technique with letters, words or objects, and move the vanishing point to different spots.

7. Be sure to notice how profoundly its placement can affect the overall drawing, and then speculate: what would someone see if he were standing *in* the vanishing point? Or further to the right or left? Remind your crew that physical location, previous experiences, background information and unspoken cues *all* add up to our individual perspectives— and that it is very possible, as multiple viewers might see your illustration, to accurately interpret "truth" in very different ways.

Activity 3

DRAWING HANDS

Ready, Set

Let's turn up the volume on this perspective stuff. One of Escher's most well-known pieces is *Drawing Hands*, in which, from wrists that remain flat drawings on a paper, two individual, dimensional hands emerge and draw one another into being. Paradoxes are amazing optical illusions; they're also pretty tricky to do well. This, however, is a take on *Drawing Hands* that anyone can do. Now that we've seen some other folks' experiments with the very subjective experience of perception, I'd say it's high time to create some trickery of our own!

Here's what you'll need:

- a ruler or straight-edge

- pencil

- a sheet of white paper

- a thin black marker

- crayons or markers in any colors.

Go!

This is a super-simple way to "lend someone a hand" by turning a 2D drawing into what appears to be a three-dimensional object. The process is really short and easy—but the effect is really cool.

1. Lay one hand on the paper with your fingers open. Using the pencil, lightly trace the outline of your hand and forearm.

2. Use the straight-edge and marker to draw horizontal lines across the paper, going right up to the hand outline, skipping over it and beginning again on the far side.

3. In marker, connect both sides of your hand, wrist and fingers with arched lines. Erase the original pencil outline.

4. Color in-between the lines. You can opt for a repeating pattern or a bold rainbow, or anything else you like!

Besides a super-cool picture, there's a bigger takeaway to talk about. Our conscious perception of the world is not static or unaffected. None of us, Aspie or otherwise, is capable of being fully objective even in our most basic observations and impressions. Our awareness of the world is constantly being informed and fine-tuned by countless factors—our mood, our confidence, our fears and desires. Being human means seeing the world through your own, constantly shifting lens. Being kind means remembering that others have fully operational lenses, too.

Activity 4

SPY GAMES

Ready, Set
Here's what you'll need:

- half a lemon

- water

- a spoon and small bowl

- a cotton swab stick or fine paintbrush

- white paper

- pencil

- tape

- marbles

- lamp, light bulb or other safe heat source.

Go!
For centuries, spies and double agents have succeeded or failed in their missions based mainly on the false impressions they were able to create. Deception. Espionage. Undercover action. Forget the James Bond stuff, real spy work was (and is!) dangerous. Lives have been saved and lost thanks to ingenious science and crafty creativity. Today, important messages make it past enemy lines via codes and sophisticated encryption software; not that long

ago, though, invisible ink was the cloak and dagger tool of the day. And so begins our own Asperkid Spy Game…

The game starts when you, the Spy Master, slip your spy team a note. Mine said:

TOP SECRET
There will be an emergency cryptography session at 1400 hours in the kitchen. Our time is limited. Our mission is grave. There are hostages.

Now, before you groan and say, "Too hokey for my kid," let me share something I learned in my days as a middle and high school teacher: the more you ham it up, the more fun even the stodgiest, cynical teen will have. If you own a trench coat, wear it. Same thing with a fedora—or maybe pencil in a mustache. The less seriously you take yourself, the more an Asperkid (or any kid) will be willing to surrender her own self-consciousness and play along.

Once our team was assembled, I explained that, "As you agents already know," cryptography is the science of ciphers (codes) and secret messages. There was, I was sorry to say, a crisis situation. A kidnapping had occurred, and the only hope of rescue lay with this team of agents. The kids were laughing—but they were totally intrigued.

Slowly, I removed a long, narrow strip of paper from my pocket. "It's a scytale" (side-uh-lee), I told them. "A transposition cipher."

Blank looks. A what? "Think about it, people. Words are usually just codes themselves. So? Crack the code." They turned to one another and examined the strip of paper. OK. *Trans* they knew meant across or change…like the Transformers (said Gavin) or transportation. And *position* was pretty clear. They had cracked it indeed. A transposition cipher is a code where the parts (usually letters, I added) are moved all around.

"Well done, team," I congratulated them. I drew out a pencil and the tape, tearing off a small piece, and affixing one end of the paper near the top of the pencil. Moving carefully, I wound the strip around and around, spiraling downward and making sure the edges of the paper touched. Once I had reached the end of the paper (near the pencil's point), I added a final piece of tape to keep it still. Then I held it up for them to see.

There, where only jumbled, random letters had been, a message appeared:

Go where you look but see different people.

"This is the first in your series of clues," I nodded seriously. And each can only be solved using this pencil—any other diameter will skew the transposition. The codes will not work. Did they understand? Yes, they agreed…and now they were getting excited.

"Each clue will lead you to a new location where we have hidden the supplies you'll need to rescue the hostages. The last one will take you to the hostages themselves. Oh!" I jumped in feigned surprise, "How could I have forgotten? The other clues are not only in code, they are also invisible."

"What? How is that supposed to work?" They wanted to know. "The process is simple—the letters will be written in acid" (I didn't say lemon juice for now…what can I say? not as dramatic). "When held near a heat

source, the heat will oxidize it and, like a browning banana, all will be revealed."

I plopped a small lamp onto the table without a shade, flicking the switch. When they needed the heat, they should hold the codes near the light bulb but NOT touch it with the paper or their hands. It would, after all, be very hot.

"Now," I shooed grandly, "off you go. Time is our enemy…"

And they were off in a mad dash to the adjacent bathroom where, they hoped, a clue might await them on the mirror…as it did, along with a hair elastic marked "Maura." That, they guessed, was the supply—odd, but OK.

Back to the lamp they came. Held near the heat, the "invisible" message I'd written earlier with the brush and lemon juice came clearly into view. They taped and wrapped the paper slip around their scytale, read the new clue and kept going.

Eventually, they had found all of the clues and "supplies" (spy "ID's" and "infrared" goggles—aka swimming goggles, etc.) and they learned who had been taken hostage and where they were being held. Heart-wrenching as it might be, the victims were…(dramatic pause) their most beloved childhood stuffed animals (gasp!) who had been dressed in embarrassingly ridiculous clothing and plopped at the end of the long upstairs hallway. Worse than that was what stood between the Spy Team and the fuzzy hostages: laser beams and land mines. OK, I might have substituted duct tape and marbles, but the adventure felt just as real.

Together, they would have to navigate over and under and around the wild criss-cross of silver tape bogging the hallway, dodging the scattered marbles and being careful not to let a stray finger or foot touch the "lasers." Each member could withstand only three "zaps" before having to return to the start of the hallway for a "first aid check" and start the precarious journey all over again.

When all spies made it to the holding room, three envelopes awaited them—one marked for each Asperkid and each containing several puzzle pieces (these were cut from a plain piece of cardboard). The trio had to assemble the jigsaw to read the final message:

Congratulations. Your teamwork has paid off. You considered invisible possibilities and have discovered great things.

The hostages are tucked under the pile of pillows in the corner and, at last check, were napping quite happily.

It turns out that they organized this little "prank" as a stunt to make us all look silly.

Oh yeah?! Just check out Spiderman in a tutu. Who looks silly NOW?? Ha! So there!

With the deepest respect,
The Spy Master

Activity 5

PLASTIC ICE CREAM TRUCKS

Ready, Set

Here's what you'll need:

- maze

- board game of strategy—chess, checkers, Rush Hour, TipOver, Mancala, etc.

Go!

Part of the downside of theory of mind trouble is that oftentimes, we Aspies will take personally that which is not meant personally, misunderstanding other people's motives and feeling insulted or attached when we needn't. What's more, we also don't realize when we are, without meaning to, making our situations worse—irritating others or coming off as arrogant or disinterested when actually, we're feeling terribly shy, insecure and desperate to be liked. I'll be honest. For an adult, it can be confusing—as though at any minute, the rug may be pulled out from under your feet. For a child, that disconnect between "my truth" and "the truth" just feels really, really sad.

Years ago I was helping my daughter work out a maze. For quite some time, she found mazes really hard. Though her vision was perfect, her eyes "jumped around" a lot, which made it difficult for her to figure out where her lines should go to get from start to finish. Visual perception challenges are, I've since learned, a common problem among many kids with ADD or ASD. It can make tasks such as handwriting, drawing, coloring and reading physically and mentally exhausting, even for folks like these two, who both sport Mensa-level IQs.

"Maura," I told her that day, "mazes, life and dinner are a lot alike." I put my finger at the end of the maze. "This is where we want to go, right?" She nodded. "Well it seems to me that if we know where we want to go and work back from there, we'll be able to see how it is we need to get there."

I asked her to imagine I was having a dinner party. From appetizers to dessert, I had planned the entire menu around having a fantastic lasagna as the main course. But in my haste, I managed to forget the ingredients for the entrée. So, the story went, I would send her to the store to "get dinner." Except, silly me, I didn't tell her what I wanted to serve. It shouldn't be a big surprise, then, that she would come home with the perfect ingredients... for beef stew. In other words, if you don't know where you are going—if you don't have a goal—how are you going to plan to get there? Similarly, if your goal is to go to an excellent university, but you don't study or work hard in school, you're not going to be admitted. If you want to make the football team and don't practice—don't do what needs to be done to get where you want to go—you won't make it.

And so we made a practice of always doing mazes backwards. It's a strategy that even now, at age ten, she employs with complicated logic and strategy games. Set your sites. What leads to that place? What leads to *that* place...and so on.

This last activity on considering perspective, then, is one you can begin with any solo maze or visual perplexor (see Resources for some favorites). Then, bump it up and include a board game like chess or checkers where you have to start considering other people's perspectives as well. My personal favorites are called Tipover and Rush Hour; I'd invite you to try using any of these as a "rear door" entrance into a tough subject. That's exactly what I did with my son.

One particular day, Sean had misinterpreted a social situation, and was feeling pretty low. The trouble, I knew, was primarily that he wasn't seeing beyond himself. He couldn't imagine a reality other than the one he had perceived. Rather than get caught up in a preachy discussion, I asked to talk about a game.

Did he remember, I asked, that we had played Rush Hour together just the day before? He did, he said. I reminded him of our game time.

The object of the game is to navigate your ice cream truck through a traffic jam to the exit. Just as in chess, mancala or checkers, the key to success is to "think before you do." Stop and plan before you act. All-in-all, a good lesson for everyone in all things. But it's especially so for Asperkids, for whom impulsivity gets them into frequent trouble. We see it every day. They speak out without thinking of the effect. They interrupt. They leave without their lunch. They turn in their homework too soon without checking their answers. In Rush

Hour, you can get yourself completely locked in on all sides, unable to escape the jam you've created simply by doing without pausing to think first. The same, I would argue, will be true for the game-playing children as they grow—in life, love and friendship.

I reminded Sean that even now, we needed to stop and think before "doing," that is, before reacting. As when we played the game, when we play with others we need to ask these three questions:

1. Who or what is in my way?

2. Who or what is in his way?

3. How much room does he need to move?

Yes, I was talking about plastic police cars and fire trucks. I was also talking about a lot more to a very young person. Personal experiences have great impact on people's opinions. The more you know about the person speaking, the better you understand why he believes what he does, what unique experiences he may be drawing upon, and what sensitive topics he may not wish to consider.

We need to ask ourselves and to teach our Asperkids to ask themselves: what is in my way of feeling content? Important? Loved? Included? Is it a thing—like a seating assignment or confusing class project that can be adjusted? Or is it a person? And if so (here's the BIG MOMENT—the theory of mind-taking, perspective-seeing challenge!), what people, problems, ideas or feelings might be keeping him or her stuck there? Maybe it's something small, and a few words will make the difference (like just moving an obstacle one position), or maybe, like the school bus, it's a bigger dilemma that requires a lot of problem-solving "space" (time, emotional room, privacy, etc.) to change.

Everyone feels that he or she is the most important, most interesting person in the world. So we have to get our Asperkids in the habit first, of wondering, "How would I feel if I were in her place? What would I want to hear?" Then, they've got to respond to what the *other* person might be feeling.

Which is why I sat there with my six-year-old and talked about Rush Hour. We talked about his day and about what had upset him. What was getting in his way of feeling happy right then and there? Asperkids often internalize their misinterpreted versions of life, turning them into feelings of isolation, worthlessness or doubt. That's where we—as parents and teachers—can make a difference.

What's in my way? What is in his way? How much room does he need to move? We discussed alternative perspectives and unconsidered obstacles. Suddenly, just by imagining a friend's perspective and the logical possibilities it included, this kiddo saw his own misunderstanding.

Because we had prepared with concrete, seeable and touchable play (and yes, it absolutely was preparation as much as it had been play)—I could use those questions to help build a case for perspective.

The power of play is limitless, and so are the children who are guided by it—both to success and to defeat. No matter what kind of child is playing, he or she is developing perspective on much more than logic, spatial-relations, visual tracking or problem solving—although each of those are worthwhile. With guidance and love, these kids are learning that their ideas matter. That their voices matter. That they matter. And that there is an awful lot you can learn about the world from a plastic ice cream truck.

Activity 6

CONSTRUCTIVE TRIANGLES

Ready, Set

Here's what you'll need:

- craft foam board or felt in yellow, green, white, blue and red

- exact-o knife or scissors

- ruler

- black marker

- plastic sandwich bags, small baskets or storage boxes

- small wooden board

- nails

- hammer

- chalk or crayons

- rubber bands.

Go!

Now, you're ready to start!

It's no secret that I'm a big fan of Montessori learning materials, largely because of the conceptual basis they provide, grounding sophisticated ideas in easily manipulated, real objects. And when we're seeking to connect part to whole and back again, you can't get better than Constructive Triangles (if I had had these, I probably would've loved geometry!).

The Constructive Triangles got their name from the idea that triangles are the first and most basic polygon, and that by combining them, we can form every other straight-edged shape. By physically having the opportunity to explore and experiment with form and geometry, Asperkids will see, touch and understand the idea of equivalence: that there are, in fact, more ways than one to reach the same end—and that each version is legitimate. In other words, each part is essential to building the whole truth, but *isn't* the whole. Moreover, it's quite possible that multiple versions of "truth" exist, depending upon one's point of view. And our Asperkids are going to begin to "get" this…from triangles.

Basics Bag (or Box)

Trace, outline and cut out the following shapes from the foam board or felt, and group them together:

1. Two congruent, green, right-angled, isosceles triangles—draw a heavy line along the hypotenuse of each.

2. Two congruent, yellow, right-angled, isosceles triangles—draw a heavy line along the *same leg* of each triangle.

3. Two, congruent, white, right-angled scalene triangles—draw a heavy line along the hypotenuse of each triangle.

4. Two, congruent, green, right-angled scalene triangles—draw a heavy line along the longest side of both triangles.

5. Two, congruent, yellow, right-angled scalene triangles—draw a heavy line along the short leg of both triangles.

6. Two, congruent, yellow, equilateral triangles—draw a heavy line along one side of each triangle.

7. One red, obtuse-angled scalene triangle *and* one red, acute-angled scalene triangle.

Present these shapes, explaining that the Asperkid should imagine the heavy lines you've drawn as being magnetic—they only stick to one another. Now, remove the yellow equilateral triangles, the white triangles and the green isosceles triangles, placing them randomly on a table.

Select a green triangle and slide the other green triangle up to meet it—using the "magnetic line" as your guide in joining the two. What have you got? A completely new shape—a square! Move the square aside, and go through the same process of assembling the two white triangles into a rectangle and the two yellow, isosceles triangles into a parallelogram. Now separate them, mix them up and let the Asperkid have a go.

Once he's got those down, present the next four pairs in the same way, building two parallelograms, a rhombus and an isosceles trapezoid, and then allowing him to do the same.

Blue Triangle Bag (or Box)

Trace, outline and cut out 12 congruent, blue, scalene right-angle triangles so that, besides the 90-degree angle, the two remaining angles measure 30 and 60 degrees (see the blue triangles in Appendix 1).

Slide together four triangles with the right angles touching, and you'll create a four-pointed star (because 4 × 90 = 360 degrees).

Keep experimenting! Make a six-pointed star with six of the 60-degree angle vertices touching. What about the 30-degree angles? How many triangles will it take to make a complete star with those meeting in the center?

Allow the Asperkid to manipulate these all-blue, no "magnetic lines" triangles. Set some "let's see what we can put together" challenges. Here are just *some* of the doable blue triangle combinations:

- a hexagon (12 triangles)

- a hexagon with a hexagonal opening in the center (six triangles)

- a rhombus (four triangles)

- a square with a "tilted" square opening in the center (four triangles)

- a crab (12 triangles).

Triangle Bag (or Box)

Trace, outline and cut out the following shapes, and group them into a third baggie or box:

1. One, large, white equilateral triangle. Then, trace this same triangle out of green, yellow and red foam board and cut those according to the following directions.

2. Two, green, right-angled scalene triangles—mirror-image of one another, heavy line marking the longest leg.

3. Three, yellow, obtuse-angled isosceles triangles where the legs of each triangle are marked with heavy lines.

4. Four, red, small, equilateral triangles. Mark one triangle with heavy lines on all three sides. Mark the other three triangles only on one side.

Present these shapes, explaining that, once again, the Asperkid should imagine the heavy lines you've drawn as being magnetic—they only stick to one another. Show him the large equilateral triangle. It represents the whole, filling a set amount of space with one large piece.

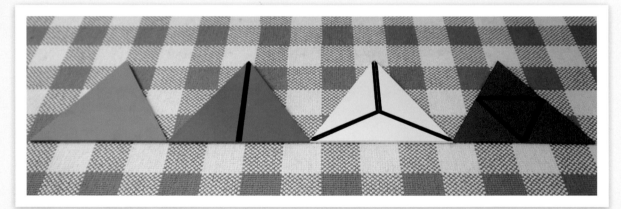

Now, slide together the two green triangles. Using two pieces, halves, you've constructed one equilateral triangle that takes up the same space as the first—lay the original on top as a tester to prove it. The methods of construction are different, but the result is equivalent.

Next, use the three yellow triangles to assemble the one, large equilateral triangle. Use the "tester"—this time, in thirds, an equal result has been attained.

And last, the four red triangles build a trapezoid and then come together as quarters of the same, large triangular space. Give the Asperkid a chance to do the same.

Then, lay them all out! Trace the triangles with chalk or crayons and extend the lines. Let the Asperkid explore the artistic possibilities, creating tessellations and tangrams (template in Resources), add color and pattern. Using any number of triangular permutations, build one hexagon next to another hexagon and then on top and below, fit more hexagons. Suddenly, it's a turtle's carapace or honeycomb from an apiary: nature's most efficient

structure. Rows of hexagons can completely tile a given volume of space using the least surface area material, equally distributing stress at each vertex, fitting together without any gaps between.

This, by the way, is a nice time to mention that bees are not aerodynamically suited for flight. Someone, however, forgot to tell the bees. So they do what they know they can do, rather than what scientific "experts" say they can do. For any kid who hears far too much about his own limitations, there's no better role model than the humble bumble bee…achieving the "impossible" every day.

Use a homemade geoboard (with guidance, safe at age three!) to evenly measure, mark and hammer rows of nails into a spare piece of wood.

Then let the Asperkid strengthen his hands as he stretches colorful rubber bands from one nail to another, recreating the triangular constructions…as well as houses, boats and anything else that comes to mind.

As you'd like, use the terms side, base, vertex and hypotenuse. They're good words to learn. Most clearly of all, however, be sure to say "different" and "equal." Why? Yes, these geometric discoveries are wonderful. They are preparatory and should

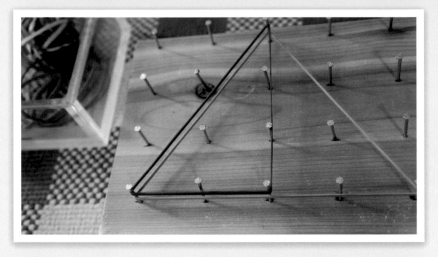

continue with creativity, curiosity and above all, with purpose. As they explore, Asperkids *see* and *feel* the reality of gestalt and of equivalence—that neither the method of subdivision nor of creation makes any result more or less valid. That is the truth of triangles, of life and of perspective. We are, in all things, both part and whole. And though we assemble our many different perceptions in many different ways, each is valid, worthy and, in the end, equal.

CAST A (PAPER) NET

Ready, Set
Here's what you'll need:

- bright cardstock in several colors

- pencil

- scissors

- glue

- string

- geometric solids (building blocks, soup cans, a book, etc.) in as many of the following as possible: cube, cylinder, cone, square pyramid, triangular pyramid, triangular prism, rectangular prism

- print outs of the polyhedron templates from Appendix 2 on the cardstock. After building stars and diamonds and crabs and whatever else the Asperkid has imagined out of triangles, let's add the third dimension. Depth specifically means how far downward, backward or inward a space is; literally, it's the distance to the opposite perspective. And in geometry, as in life, the added depth of multiple perspectives is what creates substance and beauty.

How to "Cast a (Paper) Net"

1. Start with the most basic solid—the cube. Review how many faces (flat surfaces) it has (six) and how many edges (eight).

2. Place the cube onto a piece of paper and trace the bottom face.

3. Carefully, roll it forward (keeping the edge still as you do), and trace the cube again. Roll it back to its original place.

4. Roll it toward you and trace.

5. Roll it toward you *again* and trace. Roll the cube forward twice, so it's in the starting spot.

6. Roll to the right and trace (and back) and finally, to the left, trace and back.

7. When you lift the cube off the paper, count the squares you have drawn. You've just "cast a net" for a cube, as if you had peeled a jacket off of the surface; so, you should see six adjacent faces with eight edges.

8. Draw tabs (like on a gift box) onto the top edge of the top face and around the left and right sides.

9. Finally, darken the outside edge around the entire figure—and cut the whole thing out *on the outside lines.*

10. Score and fold the interior and tab lines.

11. Run the string across the still-open net, then close and glue it together (hold for a minute or so).

Voila! Just by adding depth—another perspective, your plain plane shape has just become a three-dimensional masterpiece—not to mention your first geometric garland "bead." (And don't worry, there are templates in Appendix 2 if you want to peek!)

Now, turn the pencil, paper, scissors and glue over to the Asperkid to "cast a net" of the remaining solids. Together, talk out how many vertices, edges and faces each solid has, referring to a chart or actual object to double-check, if needed. By all means, emphasize that this activity is *not* about perfection: it's about creating something artistic and beautiful out of fixed and finite mathematics. It's discovering the fruits of new perspectives…especially when you get really fancy (as we are about to do!).

Trace or copy and cut out the Appendix 2 templates for polyhedron (shapes with many faces). Now— explore them. Take the open nets outside and play.

Sketch them—REALLY BIG! Reconstruct them with twigs. See if, together, you can recreate the rhythms, patterns, congruencies and spacing of the oh-so-carefully prepared templates.

When Gavin and I made a go of it, our driveway got crazy colorful. Using only chalk and a straight-edge, three-year-old Gavin and I counted out and then traced 20, identical equilateral triangles in the pattern that our paper template showed would create an icosahedron (adding words and rhythm to our construction: up, down, over, down); we even built a tetrahedron out of colored magnetic tiles! This, he said, was SO COOL!

Your Asperkid may be really surprised at what he can do—sensorially and kinetically building an understanding of abstract geometry theorems (the ones you and I memorized without understanding!).

Done with the chalk and tiles, Gavin and I returned to our papers, scoring and folding templates, laying the string across, tucking and glueing tabs. While the (GORGEOUS) garland was drying, we pulled with one more activity with the older kids: origami cubes. Into the center of the table went a pile of colorful, square sheets of paper measuring about 4.25 inches per side (origami paper can be purchased in any craft store, or just cut into squares from regular construction paper). And away we went!

1. Flip the colored side down, and fold the paper in half horizontally, from the top down to the bottom, carefully lining the top edge down to the bottom edge. Unfold to see a horizontal crease across the middle.

2. Now, fold each "half" in half—making quarters. Start by folding the top edge down horizontally until it meets the crease in the middle of the paper. Fold and smooth cleanly.

3. Repeat on the lower half, folding the bottom edge up to meet the center crease, then pressing and smoothing the fold.

4. Unfold the top half ONLY. The bottom stays folded.

5. Grasp the bottom left corner and lift it up and over the bottom fold, over the center line, all the way up to meet the top crease line (creating a right triangle). Press and smooth. Unfold.

6. Turn the paper 180 degrees to your right, so that the folds you just did on the left are now on the right side.

7. Refold the bottom edge up to the middle crease, and then, as before, fold the bottom left corner all the way up and over until it meets the upper crease, creating a right triangle again.

8. Leave it folded!

9. Fold down the top quarter again, bringing the top edge to the center crease.

10. Refold the top right corner along the crease you made before (the triangle you folded in Step 5). Open up the bottom quarter ever-so-slightly and tuck that top triangle into the bottom flap.

11. Flip the whole paper over. You should see a parallelogram slanting from the bottom left up to the top right with two, unfolded right triangles (one at bottom left, one at top right). Fold the corner triangles over the front side.

12. Fold in the two corners of the parallelogram to form a square (the top folds down, the bottom folds up).

13. Flip the unit over to see the two triangular pockets on the front side and the two extending triangular "tabs." These tabs will slide into the pockets of the other units you fold.

14. Once you've folded the basic unit six times, you can slip the pieces together—forming six faces, each comprised of four right-angled, isosceles triangles. (Note: if you feel ambitious, you can make an oct-ahedron with 12 of these units and an icosahedron with 30.)

Your beautiful cube assembled, it's time to check the garland. Spray it with glitter if you feel fancy, and otherwise, display your creation with pride for everyone to enjoy. After all, this Asperkid has shown perseverance, joint attention and patience. She's collaborated and tried new things.

Celebrate the process, as always, rather than the final product…and always, always look for the teachable moments—not about geometry or origami or art (although those are great, too). About having fun while touching and learning. About exploring with our fingertips. About visualizing what we feel. Recall the added beauty of adding additional perspectives and of seeking new elements, new possibilities and new points of view. And always, reiterate the grander, more enriched results that are born every time more dimensions can contribute to the overall picture.

Snapshot-Sized Fun

COSMIC CLEANUP

Ready, Set
The best kinds of messes are the ones that clean themselves up—like this homemade glow-in-the-dark bath paint. Turn off the regular lights and turn on the blacklight. Look at the world a little bit differently, and the difference is practically magic.

Here's what you'll need:

- a muffin/cupcake tin

- shaving cream

- non-toxic fluorescent paints

- paintbrushes

- blacklight bulb (any Walmart, craft or home improvement store).

Go!

1. Fill the muffin tin with plain shaving cream.

2. Add one drop of color to each cup and mix well.

3. Paint polygons on the shower door, a mural on the bottom of the bathtub, or original body art.

4. When the fun is done, the shaving cream acts as its own soap. Just rinse or wipe down!

Chapter 6

PAINT CHIP EMOTIONS

Helping Your Asperkid "See" a Rainbow of Feelings

· ·

Included Activities

1. Color Math

2. Clip the Colors Fantastic

3. Ombré Trend-ay

4. Socks and Charades

5. Planks in the Living Room

6. Not All Ick is Created Equal: Homemade Scratch-off Cards

   Snapshot-Sized Fun: Contained Color Chaos

Primary psycho-social skills
Absolutism
Emotional awareness
Emotional vocabulary

Motor and processing skills
Attention
Auditory motor integration
Auditory processing
Bilateral coordination
Cognitive
Emotional regulation
Fine motor skills
Language processing
Motor planning
Oculomotor
Problem solving
Sensory processing
Sequencing
Social skills
Visual motor integration
Visual processing
Visualization
Working memory

Teaching/learning styles
Active
Auditory
Global
Intuitive
Kinesthetic
Reflective
Sensing
Sequential
Visual

Academic enrichment and reinforcement
Language arts (spelling, speaking and listening, writing)
Math
Science
Social studies

My girlfriends and I sat rapt in the conference center audience as photographs snapped through the PowerPoint. Not long before, my daughter, husband and son had been diagnosed with Asperger's. And, like the hundreds of folks attending, I was there to learn a little something about supporting my family.

The speaker was explaining how the photos he was showing were exactly the kind displayed to adults during diagnosis. Each image featured a different social situation which, apparently, NT folks could easily assess by reading the faces and expressions of the subjects. People on the spectrum, however, had a much harder time interpreting others' feelings and intentions. I knew that already. I had seen it first-hand many times.

When Sean was two, he began attending a Mothers' Morning Out at a local preschool. Very soon after the term started, my (always-desperate-to-please) son came home and reported something strange. He was "getting yelled at," he said, by his teacher. This definitely did *not* add up. Sean is, and was, the classic Aspie rule follower. I couldn't imagine him being disobedient or rude to the adults, and no one had reported misbehavior to me. So, I asked the school staff about it.

Sean, it turned out, was not causing problems. Another child, however, was. And Sean was so sensitive to the castigation that he interpreted her corrections as being directed toward him. I understood that. As a child, I'd have to turn off TV shows when a character was about to be tricked, embarrassed or sad. It hurt too much to watch.

Maura needed emotional "tutoring," too. Once, she had run toward a street, and I'd shouted at her...bringing her to hysterical wails and tears. Why was Mommy angry? She couldn't understand. Except I wasn't angry. I was terrified.

About then, it occurred to me that an "angry" face and "scared" face could look a lot alike. An angry voice and a scared voice could sound a lot alike, too. So, we pulled out mirrors and role-played. My mom, as an onlooker, was awfully impressed. "I wouldn't have ever thought of having to explain that," she said. Really? I thought the mix-up was logical, and my response was pretty generic.

That probably should've been a clue that there was a little something different about me, too...

Back in the conference hall, the PowerPoint played on. We were supposed to look at the pictures and silently evaluate them. Then, we'd hear about the misinterpretations Aspies often made of the same photos. My friends (sitting on either side of me) smiled and nodded, taking notes as the scenarios played out. "Really?" they whispered. "That's what my spectrum kid would see in this very picture?" The other moms were fascinated. I, on the other hand, was really confused. In every single situation, I was *not* reading the emotions or dynamics that the NTs thought were obvious. My answers were matching the Aspies'.

My own diagnosis followed soon afterwards.

As nothing else ever had, this experience proved to me that we do not experience or understand emotion in the same way NTs do. So, what does life feel like for Aspies? Joyful. Confusing. It feels just like life does for you, only with the emotional "volume" turned up. And the most pervasive emotion we experience is anxiety.

Try this for me: allow your body, not just your mind, to remember a time when you felt afraid—your heart thudding, mind racing and stomach lurching. It's not a concept or idea, it's not a topic to be discussed rationally. Everything about fear is primal—irrational…and bodily. There's no logic involved.

Anxiety is one step down, but it's more exhausting in its persistence. It's a gnawing, jittery, ever-present sensation of waiting for the threat…waiting for the fear. It's like living with the *Jaws* music playing. You don't see the danger. But you surely know there's something "out there."

What most NTs don't realize is that we spectrumites, whose bodies and minds are wired differently, live with varying levels and intensities of almost perpetual anxiety. That may sound paranoid—but it's not. Paranoia is irrational fear. Most Aspies or autistics have been bullied (often many times over by children, adults and even teachers and family members), are constantly assaulted by sensory input, must fend their way daily through social situations which seem random and chaotic and often think we are at the top of our games when, in fact, the rug is about to be pulled out from under us.

Our anxiety is an absolutely rational reaction to the experiences we have. Pull at a weed and simply tear off the leaves, and what happens? Nothing new. The weed grows back. Similarly, if teachers, caregivers, therapists, spouses and friends focus their energy on tantrums and meltdowns, obsessions or rigidity, they've only torn at the leaves. Nothing will change—either in the behaviors or in the heart of the loved one.

But grab that weed near the base, dig at the roots and pull gently. What happens? Yes, another weed may grow elsewhere, but this one is gone. Anxiety is that root. It is the seed from which our topical fixations and "overly sensitive," routine-driven, black/white, obsessive behaviors arise.

We are trying to catch the rain. We are trying to create predictable order in a chaotic, often random world...by asking a million questions, by challenging exceptions to rules, by scripting dialogue we know was funny (once) or dictating play. It's not that we want to be unlikeable or difficult or dominate the conversation with topics you don't enjoy. We just want to feel secure, safe—and to be able to stop the endless waiting for unwelcome surprises.

Looking back at my own life and the life of the many other adult Aspies I've come to know, I can tell you this: in every case, we have unwittingly contributed to our own heartache. We've trusted people we shouldn't have, over-sharing intimate details with strangers who then recoil in discomfort. We've inserted ourselves into conversations and situations that did not involve us in the least. We've monopolized get-togethers, trying to relate by talking all about ourselves.

For us, the world is a social minefield, and we're walking through it with blinders on. That's the theory of mind thing again: as Mary Poppins put it, we can't see past the ends of our noses. We aren't narcissistic (in love with ourselves) or intentionally domineering, although it sure can come across that way. We bring conversations back to ourselves because that is the lens through which we try to understand everyone and everything in the world. We over-share because we're *trying* to connect. We dominate conversations and sound egocentric because we're passionate or excited about something. We learn that we must constantly be on-guard, analyzing and reanalyzing tone of voice, facial expressions, apologizing, contradicting...trying hard to recognize and integrate the "unwritten social rules" I cover at length in *The Asperkid's (Secret) Book of Social Rules* (Cook O'Toole 2013).

And you know what? It's really hard to do.

Evolutionary scientists say animals respond to fear in the way their successful ancestors learned to cope with threats. Generally speaking, mammals will first try to avoid danger, which translates for Aspies as avoiding social situations (parties, dates, job interviews), then comes depression, emotional withdrawal, keeping to ourselves at school, at work and at home. We may feel that our futures are constrained. And often, we try, as hard as we can, to fly under the radar to be unnoticeable, or to be so perfect and so commendable that no one will criticize, condemn or chastise us.

If we can't get away from social rejection, we get aggressive. It's the old "your best defense is a good offense" plan. What looks like an angry outburst or a 0–60 temper may actually be a protective reflex built upon emotional scars and real insecurities. Heightened memories of past threats will increase the wish to disappear, hide, avoid the conversation, or just flat out quit (flight). Those same memories—of feeling like a failure, unwanted or hurt—also make us quicker to anger, and with greater intensity. That's our shield. We are trying to immediately stop what feels like a threat.

This isn't crazy talk. Our fears are born of repeated exposure to very real threats either to our bodies, our minds or both. Most Aspies or spectrumites have been bullied (often many times over) or at least ridiculed for our differences. We mess up without realizing it, and then have to deal with the fallout just when we may have

thought we'd finally gotten our act together. Without a clear understanding of the whys or whens, we negotiate daily social situations that seem random and chaotic, building families, marriages and incomes upon the relationships we are able to reap in those environments.

Traumatized by real experiences, we turn to coping mechanisms that are not in line with present circumstances. We detect threats when none exist, avoiding the unfamiliar to avoid danger, hearing challenge and accusation in the voices of loved ones and interpreting sincere offers of assistance or kindness as insults and ridicule.

We think we understand others' intentions, so we are curt or avoid social situations altogether. No one will get the chance, we reason, to disappoint or hurt us. Nor, unfortunately, will they get the chance to delightfully surprise or encourage us.

As I explained in Chapter 1, we often don't communicate our own thoughts or feelings very thoroughly, either. Our intentions, reactions and designs seem self-evident. So, why bother announcing or explaining them? We assume—fast. We misinterpret—fast. We push others away—fast (or not fast enough). And in the process, we cause conflict and heartache (for others and for ourselves) that needn't exist in the first place.

So let's help Asperkids to live life less afraid. Here's what Asperkids need from you:

- **Respect the fear, don't punish self-protection.** When you feel truly scared, are you polite? Easy-going? If you know danger may very well be waiting outside the front door, would you skip and whistle on out? No. You'd do whatever or act however you needed to in order to feel safe again. That's self-preservation, and it's a GOOD thing.

- **Reconsider "misbehavior" as "missed behaviors."** Aspies will show you when we are getting nervous or trying to avoid something. Refusal to comply, fidgeting, squirminess, inappropriate silliness, rocking, lip biting or picking, cuticle picking, task avoidance or general excuses are all signs of stress.

When you see those, pay attention. This Asperkid is asking for help. If those behaviors are missed, they will quickly escalate disruptively into shouting, meltdowns, outbursts and "heels dug in" resistance. Disobedience and disrespect from an Asperkid (or anyone!) are not acceptable, of course. But when a person is afraid, that's not the time for a lecture. Take a step back and LOOK for something painful (sensory?) or scary (socially, physically or emotionally). Change that and you will change the behavior. **Show empathy and compassion, not impatience or domineering force.** That's going to get you BOTH much further than a shouting match ever will.

What else does an Asperkid need? FUN. The best way to explore anything—especially if it's difficult or uncomfortable—is through humor and subtlety.

And paint.

Activity 1

COLOR MATH

Ready, Set
Here's what you'll need:

- blue and yellow tempera or craft paints

- an ink pad

- rubber stamps or plastic refrigerator magnets of "+" and "="

- white paper

- paintbrush

- blue and yellow play-dough

- paper plate.

Go!
Asperkids see and experience the world in extremes. Right or wrong. Joyful or heartbroken. Good guy or bad guy. Best friend or cruel enemy. Disinterested or completely obsessed.

In all fairness, many NTs do the all or nothing thing, too. This humble gal's opinion is that prejudice and pigeonholing in general happen because it's easier to lump groups together, saying, "All xxxxx are xxxx," rather than taking the time and making the effort to distinguish between individuals. We often paint the world with broad, inaccurate strokes. Because, I bet you'd agree, most people, events and opportunities aren't all or nothing, black or white. They fall somewhere in the "gray" zone.

Color Me...Regal Orchid

Years ago, I worked (briefly) in the advertising world (not a good place for an Aspie, by the way). One of the worthwhile things I did pick up, though, was a knowledge of Pantone. Basically, Pantone is the standard language of accurate color communication in marketing, paper products, trademark, fashion, home design and graphic arts. I suppose it had never occurred to me how important the particulars of "green" or "pink" might be. Then again, like many Aspies, I am the first to tease apart words: do you mean "skeptical" or "cynical," "lonely" or "isolated"?

When an Aspie asks a million questions, she's not splitting hairs. She's trying to correctly decode from your words *precisely* what you want her to understand.

In the same way, Pantone assigns particular names and numbers to every imaginable color and to the exact blend of other colors which create honeysuckle, tangerine, mimosa or blue iris. That means that a designer in London can confidently order fabric from Hong Kong in 2013's Color of the Year (emerald, in case you're curious) and expect to receive the precise hue he wants. As Pantone Inc. explains, it's a universe of "color...never lost in translation."

It's long been established that color affects mood. But just maybe, I mused, it could also be used to better communicate moods. Perhaps those gradual, in-between shades could help Asperkids concretely "see" feelings. We could get them past "black and white" perceptions to much more expressive language—*à la* Pantone.

For the youngest Asperkid, the process begins by building secondary colors from primaries. And the game I designed to do that is called Color Math. It's hands on. It's concrete. And it's real. Not to mention that it's fun.

Gavin and I started out with paint in two of the three primary colors (blue and yellow), each squirted separately onto a paper plate. Before he got to play with the colors, though, I also showed him rubber stamps of "plus" and "equals" (you could use fridge magnets you don't mind dirtying) and a big ink pad. Putting the addition sign in front of him, I used what Montessorians call "the three-period lesson" to present new words:

1. Pointing to the stamp, I said, "Plus." He repeated the word two or three times. We repeated the same with "equals."

2. He closed his eyes so I could mix them up, and when he opened them again, I asked him to point to the "plus" sign. He did. I asked him to point to "equals." He did.

3. We mixed them up one last time, and then I asked him to tell me the words independently. "Plus," he said, pointing. "Equals." Great.

Now I had to make sure he knew what those words meant. I handed Gavin a small ball of both homemade blue and yellow play dough, and grabbed one of each for myself. "Ready?" I smiled. He looked at me with questioning eyes and nodded.

"Plus!" I yelled, smooshing both colors together, kneading and blending the dough balls. He could do the same, I said. And we both worked our colors thoroughly until blue and yellow had combined into a lovely green.

"What is 'plus'?" I asked, and he correctly summarized, "Put together." Yes! Without words, I had kinetically demonstrated the reality of what "plus" (and, later, "add") means.

Then, pinching off one more small bit from the yellow and blue, I put the two balls on one side of our dollar-store balance. The newly made, larger green went on the other side. It leveled out. "Equals," I announced. Gavin looked. "Equals," he repeated. "It's the same."

No abstractions. Concrete reality. Concept understood.

Last, I laid the dough balls out in a row—like a sentence. First, yellow, then the "plus" stamp, upside-down, then the blue, then the "equals" upside-down, and finally, the green. I "read" from left to right, "Yellow plus blue equals green."

"I did math!" he yelled triumphantly! Absolutely, he had. Color math.

We repeated the same process with paints, stamping in the plus and equals as Gavin painted a dollop of yellow and of blue and last, mixed a squirt of both into their "sum," green. Importantly, we varied the blending process. Once, I'd let him put yellow on the paper and then blue, then mix. The next time, he put the blue down first, then added the yellow and mixed. You might not realize it, but that's the commutative property of addition (which we also see in multiplication)—it doesn't matter in which order you add 4 + 5 or 5 + 4, or multiply 3 × 6 or 6 × 3, the answer is always the same. That's a pretty solid (and advanced) concept to teach to a little guy…but using paint and play dough, he got it, and had fun in the process.

Activity 2

CLIP THE COLORS FANTASTIC

Ready, Set

Here's what you'll need:

- paint strips from any paint or hardware store (as many as you'd like)

- a container to hold them (small pail)

- clothespins

- glue

- scissors

- ribbons, puzzle pieces, building blocks or any group of objects in different tones of the same color.

Go!

The next skill is being able to **recognize and explain comparatives and superlatives.** Academically, that's a preparatory language skill (between adjectives) and a mathematics concept involved in science, art and history. Emotionally, it's an introduction to the concept of "gray"—of levels of good and bad, happy and sad, all and nothing.

Maybe our ideas aren't the same, but they aren't necessarily polar opposites, either. That's a lesson important enough to introduce to a very young child and to remind even our "grown up" selves.

You don't need fancy supplies to begin the work. Gavin and I used a puzzle we have in which the pieces are all green rectangles. The first piece is a dark, narrow rectangle; as you move along, each additional piece becomes just a little bit wider and the tone just a little bit lighter.

But you don't need a pre-made puzzle. You can achieve the exact same set-up with several building blocks, ribbons, pieces of paper or even yarn—as long as they are all in the same color family. The concept we're teaching, in a concrete way (disguised as a game) is *non-extreme comparison.*

Put simply: **we're establishing the existence of an "er," not just the "est."**

Comparative Grading: "The 'Er' Not the 'Est'"

With your child watching, lay out the objects from darkest to lightest.

Choose any two pieces as the ones you'll compare as long as you *don't pick the lightest or darkest.* Name one "dark" and the other "darker."

Repeat the words clearly, then return the lighter to the original group.

Choose an even darker object to bring out. Now, what had been "darker" is actually lighter. Point to the now-lighter piece, and call it "dark." Indicate the new piece, naming it "darker." Return them to the group. You've just demonstrated that colors (and later, other things, too) are not absolute: they exist in comparison to one another. Similarly, a bad day on vacation is still better than the best day of having the flu.

Ask the Asperkid to choose two ribbons or papers, etc. and to please show you the "dark" and then "darker." Move *either* back to the group, requesting he choose any "darker."

Can he name which is which? The last round, you pick out the objects again, but ask the Asperkid to do all of the naming.

Superlative Grading: "The 'Est'"

Putting away the puzzle pieces, I brought Gavin a new game that I had made using color strips from the paint store and some old-fashioned wooden clothespins.

Beforehand, I had cut each strip lengthwise, so that I would have a bit of each color to use while using the actual color gradation intact. Then, I'd snipped a small square of each hue and glued one square to the end of each clothespin.

Now that everything was dry, I clipped each pin to the top lip of a small pail full of the paint chips, and brought the whole thing out to my little guy (and his big brother, who is always curious to see what's going on).

Gavin loves (or is possessively obsessed with, depending upon how you'd like to describe it), all things blue. So, the only logical start was with the strip of blues and the clothespins that would match.

1. I pulled out the paint strip and unhinged the blue clips, laying them all before him.

2. Choosing the clothespin with the middle tone, I slowly moved it along the paint strip, comparing it visually to each color as I moved down the *whole* line. Yes! I concluded after checking all of my options, the clothespin's blue matched the middle color.

3. I opened the clip and held the paint strip in my "helper hand," demonstrating how to match and attach the two. "This blue [pointing to the color I had just identified] is darker than this blue [indicating the lightest hue]."

4. Then, I turned and asked, "Could you please find the color that is dark but not darker?" Gavin immediately pointed to the lighter color. Good, now could he choose and attach the correct clothespin to that spot? Yes!

5. Could he then, please point to "dark"? He did. What about "darker"? Bingo! And last, could he clip on the "darkest" blue? With only one remaining, he moved quickly and confidently. He had it.

6. The second time we played, I started by asking him to find the "darkest" first. Then, indicating the remaining clips, which was "darker"? He found it and matched the clothespin. By process of elimination, only "dark" was left.

7. Extend this game with as many color strips as you would both like—branching to other comparisons and superlatives (the extremes). You can compare anything from perfume scents (nice, nicer, nicest) to leaf sizes (long, longer, longest).

You can make the experience more complex, too. Maura and I, in preparation for her black light "neon" birthday party, baked cookies in the shape of a neon molecule.

Which electron shell had more electrons than the third shell (which has zero)? Which had the most? Which were there most of: electrons, protons or neutrons?

Regardless of age, the only parameter at this point in skill development is to make sure your child is evaluating real, concrete things. That's the foundational (and reinforceable) skill she'll need to generalize this skill to greater and greater abstractions as she grows.

Advanced Color Theory

If an Asperkid is ready to advance the discussion now, go for it. Explain that, as I mentioned earlier, scientists have shown that colors can affect our moods. For instance, a blue room actually lowers blood pressure. A red room increases tension. There seems to be a direct connection between color and feeling.

As you can both plainly see in the blends you've just created, most colors in the world are "in-between" colors; they're not "all" one thing or "all another." The same is true of feelings. It's important to remind kids that—almost ALL the time—however they feel, however Mom feels, however the teacher or kids at school seem to feel, almost nothing is actually as "black or white," as all or nothing as it seems. Maybe an Asperkid has been bullied: does she truly know, then, that not everyone "hates" her? Or maybe a good friend has let him down. One mistake doesn't a friendship break. **Colors aren't all or nothing. Neither are days, people or situations. It's easier to be absolute about anything—but "absolute" is usually absolutely wrong.**

Let's see—really see—what else might be possible, other than just happy, sad, mad, scared…those are boring, lazy words anyway. Yes, it takes more time and thought to decide that someone is insecure rather than plain scared. But it sure goes a lot further towards understanding him and effectively responding to him.

Make the effort. Choose a red family from the color strips, for example, and on the back (or on a piece of masking tape you place above it), write "ANGRY" in black marker. Now, using a fine point marker or pen, label the lightest red clothespin "jealous," the middle color "frustrated" and the darkest shade "angry."

Ask the Asperkid to describe what she thinks each adjective means. Share your own stories of times when you each felt those feelings. What caused them? How did your body feel at the time? How did you handle your emotions? How do you wish you had?

Most importantly, listen—don't take over the conversation. Be really honest about your own failures and less-than-fabulous moments. **You're not impressive when you're false and perfect. You're only a role model when you're honest, fallible, human…and still trying.**

Want some more words to help enrich those clothespins? On a three-level scale (the most common strips I saw in our hardware store), try these:

Color family	Broad label	Light tone	Medium tone	Darkest tone
Yellow	Happy	Playful, amused, interested, optimistic.	Cheerful, energized, hopeful, excited.	Joyful, thrilled, delighted, ecstatic.
Blue	Peaceful	Grateful, responsive, calm, secure.	Trusting, caring, thoughtful, worthwhile.	Loved, loving, content, valued.
Purple	Sad	Remorseful, "stupid," worn out, isolated.	Apathetic, bored, exhausted, ashamed.	Guilty, depressed, lonely, heartbroken.
Orange	Scared	Embarrassed, inadequate, discouraged, overwhelmed.	Confused, unwanted, helpless, anxious.	Rejected, overpowered, frightened, terrified.
Green	Empowered	Confident, valuable, worthwhile, successful.	Important, appreciated, respected, wanted.	Proud, talented, essential, heard.
Red	Angry	Jealous, skeptical, irritated, distant.	Frustrated, hurt, critical, selfish.	Angry, hostile, hateful, aggressive.

Activity 3

OMBRÉ TREND-AY

Ready, Set
Here's what you'll need:

- wooden cubes (craft stores sell bags full)

- white paint

- any other colors you'd like

- paint brushes

- paper plate or empty egg carton

- painter's or masking tape

- Lego bricks—all the same size (21 of the same color, 15 white)

- permanent marker

- tongs

- the color chart from Advanced Color Theory

- stapler or sewing equipment

- six toothpicks.

Go!

From nail polish to wedding cakes, hair coloring to fashion runways, ombré is everywhere. If somehow you've missed the "it" trend, ombré (pronounced "ämbrā") is where, from one end of the fabric, hair strand or confection to the other, a color progresses gradually in tone from dark to light. In total honesty, when I created these games, I wasn't doing it to be consciously *de la mode*. But hey, if I can teach a concept, have fun and be trendy: that's a no-brainer, thanks. I'll take it.

So, we know that every other color is some blend of primary colors. After all, most of what we see isn't pure red, blue or yellow. Mostly, we see secondary and tertiary combinations: lilac and cyan, vermillion and fuchsia. Feelings, too, are composites of others. "Sad," for example, might be a little bit of disappointment plus some loneliness and a dash of boredom. "Scared" may actually be overwhelmed, mixed with confused and discouraged.

Usually, there's a better word we can use to describe how we feel about something than happy, sad or mad. If we were doing a science experiment, and the precise amount of iron needed was 12.5g, would 14g be "close enough"? Of course not! Is calling a cube a square "close enough" to be right? Nope. What about dubbing something scarlet that's actually just bubble-gum pink? There are steps "in between" almost everything: numbers, colors, theories, opinions and feelings. **If we're going to empower our kids to discern others' feelings and more productively communicate their own, we have to help them discover the graded ingredients within the "colors" of emotion.**

This is really a topic that can be adapted to any age. And here's what you do:

1. Bring out the Lego bricks. Ask the Asperkid to help you build six towers—for discussion's sake, let's say we're using orange and white. Every tower will contain six bricks: the first is all orange, the second is five orange with one white on top, then four orange and two white, three orange and three white, two orange and four white, and last, one orange and five white. Then, line them up so that from the Asperkid's viewpoint, from left to right (as he reads) they go from orange to most white.

2. Rip off a small piece of the tape and lay it vertically on the table in front of each tower. Explain that because each tower has six pieces in total, you'd like the Asperkid to write a "6" on the bottom of each piece of tape in permanent marker.

3. When she's done, draw a small horizontal line above each "6." "Now, we're going to record our recipe," you should explain. "We are going to write down how many bricks in each tower are orange. Only orange." Hence, the Asperkid will write "6, 5, 4, 3, 2, 1."

4. Review. Which number on each strip tells us how many bricks there are in the *whole* tower? (The bottom; aka the "denominator" in the fractions they've just written!) And which number tells us the part of the whole tower that's made up of orange bricks? (The top; aka the "numerator.") You can name those words if you want to; more important is understanding the idea of part and whole as either a fraction (or, if your Asperkid knows fractions but hasn't worked much with ratios, record the information comparing orange to white, rather than orange to all. That would be 6:0, 5:1, 4:2, 3:3, 2:4, 1:5).

5. Here is where you might begin making analogies to more abstract notions. For example: "This all-orange tower sort of reminds me of the perfect day. It's 'all' good. Ice cream for breakfast, a long walk, a great book…what else would you add?" After soliciting their input, I'd point to the middle of the line, where the tower is equal-parts orange and white. "Maybe this day is so-so. Half-and-half. We got a flat tire but won a free pizza. I stubbed my toe hard, but got I giant surprise hugs from my kids." And the last one, well, that's one of those days you'd pretty much rather forget. Everything seemed to go wrong, and you're just glad it's done. Why, then, is there still one "good" brick, even in the lousy day? Simple. Because even on the worst day, there is always, always, always something to be thankful for.

6. Now, it's time to paint, following the "recipe" you've just written. Each "color set" requires six cubes. Just decide if you want to paint one face of each cube (easily done by taping off one side) or the whole block.

7. Six healthy squirts of the solid color paint go into one end of an empty egg carton or onto a large paper plate, followed by five squirts of color and one white, four squirts of color and two white…and so on as the brick labels dictate. Then, use a separate toothpick to thoroughly blend each "puddle."

8. Paint the taped-off face of one wooden cube (or the whole cube if you'd like), one cube per hue. Let dry. Make additional color sets as you'd like (the more the better).

9. Once they are dry, mix the cubes (and with multiple sets, invite the Asperkid to sort blues from pinks or yellows from browns).

10. Then, carefully compare each block to the group, deciding, one at a time, is it darker than this cube? Or this cube? Or this cube? Line them up from darkest to lightest, six per set. And, if a change has to be made, let the Asperkid lead the charge, solving any errors independently—unless you see real frustration mounting.

11. For bonus points, offer different kinds of tongs (sugar, wooden, berry) and the challenge to stack each color family into a tower from darkest to lightest (or the other way around).

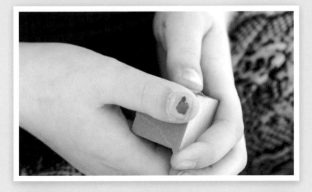

Feelings—heck, even life in general—is more like a range than an either/or, just like the blocks. We all have good days and bad days. But most are somewhere in-between. When we react to people and events, we have to be very careful not to jump from one end to the other, from 0–60, skipping every other possibility for problem-solving, sharing and personal connection along the way.

Ask that your kiddo retrieves the same colors used on the blocks to paint a smudge of each, going from darkest to lightest, on a sheet of paper. Be sure to leave room next to each color where she can write.

Now pull out the color chart from the Advanced Color Theory activity.

Next to each gradation of paint on the paper, let the Asperkid choose a feeling word to match, and write in the "labels" of choice.

After completing a few sets, staple or sew the sets into a personalized **"Colors of Emotions"** booklet. Practice using the booklet as a guide to understanding one another better (that means you use it, too!).

Ask, rather than deciding, from day-to-day: is he overwhelmed or insecure? Confident or proud? Relaxed or thoughtful? Use the concrete visual of the ombré

color pages to help connect the Asperkid to others' feelings, too.

How can we support someone who feels jealous or celebrate with someone who feels excited? Begin in calm moments, and eventually, try to use it as a way to manage tenser times—of anxiety or shame. By clearly identifying his own feelings, the Asperkid will be more effective in asking for or acquiring the support he needs without melting down, lashing out or hurting those who want to help.

Activity 4

SOCKS AND CHARADES

Ready, Set
Here's what you'll need:

- old, unmatched socks

- a pair of dice

- scoops, pitchers and bowls

- small soda or water bottles

- scissors

- rice, dried beans or popcorn kernels

- chalk

- a trampoline, if available

- index cards

- crayons.

Go!

It was a holiday weekend. For most families, that means unstructured luxury. But for those of us on the spectrum (and our kids!), unstructured time brings boo-koos of anxiety. It's runaway thinking time. What should I be doing? Am I forgetting something? Am I going to get dragged to another noisy party or mall or holiday dinner full of strangers?

Routines are disrupted. Activities are on hiatus. Homework requires even more self-discipline to tackle than usual (Monday seems SO far away!). As the parent, keeping routines as similar as possible is, of course, helpful. Then again, holidays have their own precious routines—I can't overstate the value of family traditions (for all kids, but especially for Asperkids, who will see traditions as their own short-term, still-known bit of "familiar"). That being said, we all know that peacefully raising a spectrum kiddo requires extra adult preparation. It's tough. It's tiring. I get it. But it's required if you want to keep meltdowns and sibling warfare to a minimum. My husband works all through the holiday and the weekend—so I'm home with three Asperkids under 11. Believe me, I know this is not easy.

On that particular day, Mom (desperate for something to stop the in-fighting) raided the most underused resource in any home— the "pair-less sock bag." Out came 12 lonely, largely outgrown crew socks (no short socks for this project). I doled out rice, dried beans and popcorn kernels, each offered in its own walled container, along with miniature scoops, pitchers and bowls for transferring.

Next, I sliced the top third off some plastic juice and soda bottles. These would be our large-mouthed funnels. Each kiddo then began filling the socks, using their

"helper hand" to hold open the sock while inserting the "funnel," then scooping, pouring or spooning the grains into the socks.

They had to negotiate the trials of bilateral coordination (using each hand to simultaneously do different tasks at once), dexterity in filling and then "wringing" the kernels down, folding the tops over and finally, tying (or trying to tie) a knot before pulling the top of the socks down and open over the new "bean bag." What to do with these new creations? Sky's the limit!

Gross motor? Play catch (or "nail your sibling," as it became)…balance/posture races…corn hole (tossing them through hoops or rings or into buckets). Or try what we did and mix up the mental and the physical.

To practice hand-eye coordination, depth perception and a little bit of strategy (not to mention those pesky "math facts"), we drew chalk "dividend" squares on the pavement.

1. Each player uses colored chalk to draw a giant "Bingo board" on the pavement. Then, the players are allowed to fill in each of the "spaces" with any multiple of the numbers 1–12. It could be 42, 81, 25, 144—the player chooses how to fill in his/her "board."

2. Next, in turns, each child tosses the dice and must identify which (if any) of the numbers they've written on the pavement are a multiple of their roll. For example, if a player rolled two sixes (totalling 12), she could scan her "board" for 144, 24, 60, or other any multiple of 12.

3. Once a player successfully spies and announces a multiplication fact ("There are 36! 12 x 3 makes 36!") or its division equivalent ("There are 36! 36 divided by 3 is 12!"), he tosses a bean bag onto the square to "claim" it—trying to score a straight line…

You'll recall my story earlier about misinterpreting facial expressions. Well, the problem has a much bigger impact on daily life than you probably realize if it doesn't affect you. That's why we, at *chez* O'Toole, made a little game out of the confusion.

In the Feelings Charade version of Socks and Charades, we drew a chalk hopscotch board on our enclosed backyard trampoline—more bounce equals more sensory input, which equals more fun AND more calming effect.

Before calling the kids, I labeled index cards with feeling words: AFRAID, HAPPY, ANGRY, EMBARRASSED, PROUD, SURPRISED, COMPASSIONATE, CARING. The kids and I acted out what we thought each one looked like, and along the way, I made particular reference to some of the clues that help to distinguish between a few common confusions. Then, the plan goes as follows:

1. Draw a traditional hopscotch board on pavement or a trampoline, and toss the sock bean bag onto Square 1, where it has to land and stay without touching the edges or bouncing out. If the player's sock doesn't make its mark, the turn goes to the next player. If it stays put, the player jumps over the square onto Square 2.

2. Only one foot is allowed in a square at a time. Strictest, classic rules (apply as your kids are able) say that your foot has to stay in the square without touching the lines or letting the other foot touch the ground, or you lose your turn.

3. At the end of the board, turn around and hop back in reverse order. Once the player reaches the square before the sock, he must lean down and pick it up.

4. In our version, the jumper is allowed to put both feet down at this point. I then whispered a "feeling" name into the player's ear, which had to be acted out for the others to guess (the charade part).

5. When they guessed the emotion in play, the jumper was allowed to hop over the square, completing their turn. To keep everyone engaged, the next player went right away. And in the next round, the sock goes to Square 2. You can decide either that the whole group wins once everyone has made it through all ten squares, or that the first person to make it through the entire course successfully wins, depending upon the tolerance levels of the kids.

Here's a handy list you might like to use when creating your own "charade":

Emotion	Often confused with	Clues to notice
Fear	Surprise	When someone is afraid, his jaw drops and the mouth hangs open. The eyebrows are relatively flat. When he's surprised, though, they arch and open much wider.
Happiness	Politeness	A genuinely happy smile happens around the eyes. Facial muscles tighten, making little wrinkles around the sides. That's your sign that a person isn't just smiling politely; he's sincerely happy about something.
Embarrassment	Amusement	When a person feels embarrassed, he averts his gaze. Often, he moves his head down and to the side. Also, an embarrassed smile is different from other smiles: lips are pressed together instead of being relaxed and broad.
Pride	Happiness	Someone who feels proud will tilt his head back, slightly jutting out his jaw. That's a sign of power—he's not just feeling glad, he's feeling strong and in control.
Compassion	Sadness	Eyebrows are pulled in and up, and the head tilts forward slightly. When a person feels compassionate, his lips press together; when he feels sad, his lips pull down.

Activity 5

PLANKS IN THE LIVING ROOM

Ready, Set

Here's what you'll need:

- pillows or cushions

- a wooden plank or board

- an empty plastic storage tub

- a small step stool

- popsicle sticks.

Go!

My dad passed away seven years ago from lung cancer. On many occasions, he tried to quit smoking. He would stop, and then, furious with himself for his "weakness," he'd fail and start again. I remember how discouraged he would be, so mad at himself. But the last time it happened, I put my hand on his and said, "No, Daddy, you're just expecting to succeed without a replacement coping mechanism."

The fact was—and still is—that every one of us has bad habits that we use to get through life's pitfalls. For some, it's cigarettes. For others, it's drinking an extra glass of wine, sneaking a late-night bowl of ice cream or putting away a whole box of cookies…without help. We all tell ourselves, "Never again."

But life will always, always have unforeseen stressors in store. Maybe it's an annoying coworker or a surprise bill. Maybe it's another email from school to have to manage. Unless we have prepared specific ways to handle the stress, the only way we know to get through it is the go-to standby. It sounds trite, but you know the line: fail to plan, and you plan to fail.

Asperkids are no different. You may find, as we have in our house, that sometimes they choose less-than-fabulous coping strategies, too. Usually, if an Asperkid breaks rules, they do so rather, well, badly. That is, obviously. We Aspies are notoriously bad liars and leave trails of clues everywhere. There's not a lot of slick stealth going on. But. It doesn't mean Asperkids, like any kids, won't try to be sneaky—and they will *not* understand the possible consequences of the choices they make. If an Asperkid is routinely choosing dangerous, inappropriate or disallowed methods of handling stress, know this: unless you provide viable alternatives, he will continue to choose those methods for want of a better option.

Demonstrate it.

1. Bring the Asperkid into a space where you will already have pushed the large, empty, open storage container up to a couch (or sturdy elevated surface) and, on the floor, surrounded it with cushions and pillows.

2. Lay the plank across the open container from the couch to the opposite end. Place the step stool there, on the ground.

3. Invite the Asperkid to climb up onto the couch.

4. Explain that the storage tub is stress—maybe it's a particular issue that's bothering your child, maybe it's something

generally bothersome, like a crowded party or itchy tag. Maybe it's peer pressure or impulsiveness.

5. The board represents the way she chooses to get across the rough patches. First, explain, it stands for whatever the not-so-hot method has been. Ever so slightly, tilt the board, and tell her to walk across (that's why the pillows are there at the ready if she wobbles). She will make it across, but ask her if it felt safe. The answer *should* be "no." Because it isn't safe. Whatever bad choices are being made to get through the stress are *not* alright.

6. Bring her back up onto the couch. Take away the board. "OK," challenge her, "come on across." Of course, she can't get across. There's no "bridge"—she'd fall on her face trying to jump. Point made. Without a different coping strategy, she can make all the promises in the world and have the best of intentions…but she's going to fall.

7. Together (it's really important that she is invested in this process), generate a new "plank," a new choice that would be realistic and healthy. Lay the board solidly across the tub, and let her walk. Confidently.

8. Do the same thing two or three more times until you've come up with several different options— "planks"—physically inviting her to walk across "on" each choice.

9. Provide her with popsicle sticks on which you've written her new "planks." These are pocket-sized reminders of the good ideas that she helped to imagine and which you can assure her are safe, appropriate options for managing stress.

Above all, through it all, shower her with explicitly spoken, unconditional love that says, "I may be disappointed. I may be angry. I may be hurt. I may not like what you've done. But I will always, always love you."

Activity 6

NOT ALL ICK IS CREATED EQUAL: HOMEMADE SCRATCH-OFF CARDS

Ready, Set

Asperkids can have a VERY hard time teasing apart one feeling from another. When insecurities, comparisons and self-esteem play in, it can be tough to let your heart distinguish "angry" or "critical" or even "generally frazzled" from a "mean, personal attack." Feeling under fire, Asperkids naturally retreat into anxiety, isolation and depression (flight), say impulsively cruel or mean things (more often girls), or get unnecessarily aggressive (fight). We've got to help them to distinguish more accurate perceptions and prepare more appropriate responses.

Here's what you'll need:

- adhesive bandage and baby-oil-soaked cotton ball

- sandpaper (coarse is better)

- something "pokey" although not dangerous—the tines of a fork, a toothpick, etc.

- a pile of heavy books

- dish soap

- acrylic craft paint, any color you like

- black marker

- paint brush

- packing tape

- painter's tape

- three index cards or pieces of quarter-page cardstock.

Go!

1. Mix together a 2:1 paint to soap recipe. Stir thoroughly but slowly—you don't want bubbles.

2. Hold each index card vertically, writing the following words in quotes in black marker—just as they appear:

   a. Top half: "I AM SO ANGRY! I CANNOT BELIEVE YOU JUST DID THAT! GO TO YOUR ROOM, I can't even look at you right now."

      Bottom half: "Angry," "Loud," "Mean/To punish/Scare."

   b. Top half: "No, no. Everything's fine. But just wait until I tell everyone what you did. We'll see if you have any friends by lunchtime."

      Bottom half: "Angry," "Calm Tone," "Mean/To Intimidate."

   c. Top half: "I feel really angry at what you just did, and my feelings are really hurt. I need some space right now, so please go to your room until I call you to come talk."

      Bottom half: "Angry," "Calm Tone," "Not Mean—Build Honest Relationship."

3. Tape the cards on the top and bottom edges with painter's tape.

4. Cover the bottom halves of the index cards with clear packing tape, smoothing out any bubbles.

5. Using thin layers (it usually takes a few!), paint over the packing tape until you can't see the print anymore.

6. Once everything is dry, very carefully peel the painter's tape from the top and bottom edges of the cards.

7. Wrap any extra bits of packing tape around the back, so the sides are crisp.

8. Ta-da! You've just made your own scratch-off cards!

9. Draw this table on a window, mirror or white board with dry erase marker (or use paper if you feel less adventurous). Then TOGETHER (we're going for experiences in success!), help the Asperkid fill in his responses (this makes a great group activity if you make enough cards).

	Tone/facial expression/ body Cues: angry? Not angry?	Made me feel ____ when I heard it.	Volume: loud? Calm?	Intention?
a)				
b)				
c)				

10. Use a pen to draw a sad face on your own hand. Then, cover it with the bandage strip, and explain:

- Anger is a band-aid emotion. It's real. There it is. I can see it, feel it. But the problem to be solved or healed isn't the band-aid…it's what's underneath.

- Anger has to be softened, like a band-aid, to come off without force. (Dab a little bit of oil on a cotton ball and loosen the adhesive. Pull off the bandage gently.)

- Only once the anger is gone will we discover the "feeling" wound—usually shame, insecurity, embarrassment or rejection—that is being hidden by the anger.

- Once the anger is out of the way, we can listen, talk and heal the hurt…with no more need for that "protective" bandage layer.

Onto the Cards!
Card A:

- Read the card ALOUD; the all-caps section should be forceful, and a bit aggressive.

- Guide the Asperkid to watch your clues that someone is angry: raised voice, closely drawn eyebrows, whether you lean in or stand much higher than him, if your eyes squint, if you slightly shake your head "no" from side-to-side at any point (do all of these!).

- Ask: "Was my voice loud or calm?" (Volume: loud.)

- "Did I sound angry or not angry?" (We're going for "yes!") "Why or why not?" Record the answer.

- Reread the statement. "How did you feel when I spoke to you that way? What were you thinking?" (Frequent answers: scared, panicky, uncertain, small.)

- "If someone speaks to you in a loud, angry voice that makes you feel scared, does he want to work together to make things better?" (NO!) The goal of being mean is to hurt, embarrass or frighten someone. (This tactic is more common among, though certainly not exclusive to, boys and men.)

- Now, take the fork and poke the Asperkid (with warning). Don't be too rough, but you do need to make the point that she feels some discomfort. Explain that words spoken in this way "hurt," just as if we were feeling physical pain.

- SCRATCH OFF THE CARD AND MATCH YOUR ANSWERS.

Card B:

- Read the card ALOUD; speak slowly and deliberately. You may even whisper. Add an "edge" to your tone.

- Guide the Asperkid to watch for *other* clues that someone is angry: a piercing glare that bores straight at you, getting "too close" so you can still hear their low-volume (do all of these!).

- Ask: "Was my voice loud or calm?" (Volume: calm.)

- "Did I sound angry or not angry?" (We're going for "yes!") Note together that a calm voice CAN be an angry voice—angry can be quiet, too.

- Reread the card. "How did you feel when I spoke to you that way? What were you thinking?" (Frequent answers: intimidated, threatened, worried, bullied, alone.)

- "If someone speaks to you in a quiet, angry voice that makes you feel threatened or intimidated, does she want to work together to make things better?" (NO!) The goal of being a bully is to isolate, frighten and weaken someone. (This tactic is more common among women and girls, who often bully "subtly," less physically and more mentally.)

- Again, with warning, use the sandpaper as an abrasive on the Asperkid's arm. You don't want to cause actual pain, of course, but you do want to illustrate legitimate discomfort. Like the spoken words, this doesn't "feel good," either.

- SCRATCH OFF THE CARD AND MATCH YOUR ANSWERS.

Card C:

- Read the card ALOUD; speak slowly and deliberately. You should sound serious, take a deep breath or two as you try to "keep your cool."

- Guide the Asperkid to watch for *even more* clues that someone is angry: avoiding eye contact, even their closing eyes, perhaps crying.

- Ask: "Was my voice loud or calm?" (Volume: calm.)

- "Did I sound angry or not angry?" (We're going for "yes!") Note together that, as before, a calm voice CAN be an angry voice—BUT there is a qualitative difference to the calm.

- Reread the card. "How did you feel when I spoke to you that way? What were you thinking?" (Frequent answers: regretful, sad, worried, mad at myself, uncomfortable, embarrassed.)

- "When someone speaks to you in a quiet, calm voice that tells you how *he* feels as the result of your action (called an "I statement"), instead of calling names or insulting you, is *that* being mean?" (No.) "Why?"

- Give the Asperkid a stack of heavy books to hold for as long as she can. Then, once she is fatigued but not hurting, help her put them down one at a time. It's not easy to realize that you've hurt, upset or disappointed someone. It doesn't feel good either—but if you pay close attention, the feeling is closer to the weight of the books against your stomach. You may even feel sick. And you certainly may WANT to "fight back," try to cause hurt or even run away. DON'T DO IT! Listen. Reflect. And respond to her *feelings*, not to your version of the facts.

- When someone cares enough about you to honestly, carefully share her feelings, she's demonstrating that she values you enough to trust you, even now. That's a person who cares about maintaining or even building a friendship—greeting her show of respect with an insult, barb, argument or threat will risk the entire relationship. And this sounds like one you don't want to lose.

- SCRATCH OFF THE CARD AND MATCH YOUR ANSWERS.

Note to Asperkids: angry and mean are NOT the same things. There are lots of kinds of "icky" feelings…embarrassment, regret, fear, sorrow, unworthiness…it never feels good to know we've upset someone. But, like the physical discomfort of the fork, sandpaper and heavy books, fear, humiliation and regret are actually very different kinds of discomfort. Practice distinguishing one from the other, being certain to match your response to the situation you're truly facing.

Snapshot-Sized Fun

CONTAINED COLOR CHAOS

Ready, Set
One day, serve a little something different on the dinner table.
 Here's what you'll need:

- large, zip-top bags

- multiple colors of tempera or craft paint

- optional: glitter, or use glitter paints

- painter's tape.

Go!

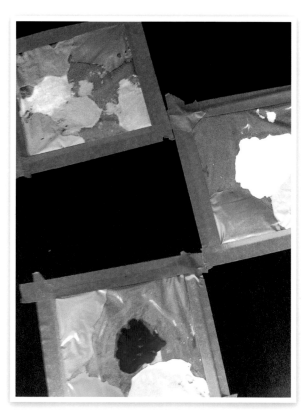

1. Squirt different colors of paint into individual pockets of a bag, taking care to try to avoid blending the colors as you close the top and squeeze out the air.

2. Lay the bag gently on the table. Tape all four edges down.

3. Time for mess-free fun. Blend the paints without touching them…then use fingertips (not fingernails!) to draw and write. Make handprints, object outlines. Or, sprinkle play sand onto glue lines on cardstock. Make homemade sandpaper letters or cartoons, and slip the papers under the paint bags for handwriting practice!

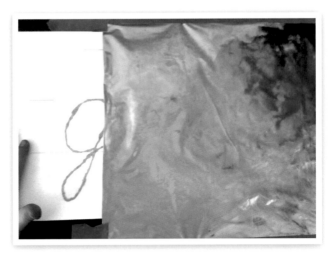

Chapter 7

CRACKING, POKING AND POPPING

Breaking Through Rigidity and Letting Wonder In

....

Included Activities

1. Fried Marbles

2. Good Clean Fun: Petri Dishes, Geodes and Popsicles

3. Permissible Breakthroughs: Nine Ways to Play with Bubble Wrap

4. Pomanders, Tattooed Bananas and Constellations

5. Snapshot-Sized Fun: Slime. 'Nuff Said

Primary psycho-social skills

Flexible thinking
Reciprocity
Resistance to change

Motor and processing skills

Attention
Auditory motor integration
Bilateral coordination
Cognitive
Emotional regulation
Fine motor skills
Language processing
Motor planning
Problem solving
Sensory processing
Sequencing
Social skills (turn taking)
Visual motor integration
Visual processing
Visualization
Visual-verbal
Working memory

Teaching/learning styles

Active
Auditory
Global
Intuitive
Kinesthetic
Reflective
Sensing
Sequential
Visual

Academic enrichment and reinforcement

Language arts (spelling, speaking and listening, writing)
Math
Science
Social studies

Cognitive rigidity: two words you probably don't hear every day. But if you live with an Asperkid, I can promise that you experience them.

Basically, "cognitive rigidity" means inflexible thinking. The "it-has-to-be-this-way-or-I-might-completely-lose-my-mind" sort of anxious reaction that is the uber-classic Aspie response to change, deviation…anything that feels chaotic and, therefore, threatening. Frequently, I refer to this as being like "uncooked spaghetti." Not too pliable. And, in fact, when bent just a little bit—SNAP! Game over.

Call it the mighty oak versus the flexible willow; call it uncooked spaghetti or cognitive rigidity. It doesn't matter. The issue of inflexibility stems from anxiety and loss of control. Dig beneath the anxiety with the strategies we've just covered in Chapter 6. Then, find some clever ways to show that poking through the expected *can* cause breakdowns…or breakthroughs. It all depends upon the choices they make.

Activity 1

FRIED MARBLES

Ready, Set
Here's what you'll need:

- glass marbles

- a metal muffin or cake tin

- oven

- bowl of very icy water

- small tongs

- towel

- bell cap, jump ring (from the jewelry aisle of any craft store)

- chain necklace, keychain OR long, thin ribbons

- super glue

- pliers.

Go!
For millennia, miners and stone masons the world over have relied on a very simple technique called "thermal shock" to do what brute strength and sharp tools could not: crack through enormous, solid rock. It's one of the secrets of Egypt's ancient pyramid builders

and a common practice even in modern day quarries. By exposing the rock to extreme and sudden change in temperature, engineers can cause great fissures to fracture otherwise impenetrable surfaces. No dynamite required. Just drastic change.

This is a great story to share with an Asperkid who has started to become aware of his or her own extreme reactions to upset plans or just to "stress" in general. He is like the glass marble you'll show him. Transparent. Honest. Beautiful. And not particularly malleable. Go ahead. Have him step on that marble without shoes. Not fun. For a small thing, the marble, like an Asperkid, can be pretty rigid—pretty tough.

Let's experiment, shall we? Let's see what happens when we force the marble to experience dramatic change.

1. Preheat your oven to 450 degrees Fahrenheit and, when ready, place a marble into each muffin cup (or put the whole lot into a cake pan), and then stick the lot straight into the oven for seven minutes.

   Get your metal bowl filled with very, very icy water, and set it near the oven.

2. As soon as the timer goes off, remove the tin from the oven and, using the tongs, drop the marbles one-by-one into the icy water. BE SURE TO STAND BACK A BIT as you do this part.

3. What's happened? Heating the glass caused it to expand unevenly. The rapid thermal shock of the icy water caused uneven shrinkage. Put the two forces together, and the resulting stress causes (very beautiful) fissures and fractures within the glass, although the surface of the marble (usually) stays intact.

Like marbles, people may look "whole" on the outside, but when we are rigid in the face of change or stress, everything and everyone weakens…and cracks. We only remain solid and strong by adapting gradually, rather than resisting absolutely (as we'll see in our next activity).

Once you've finished your sciencey craft, consider using your "shattered" or "fried" marble as a wearable or sharable reminder of the experience—and of the intrinsic lesson.

4. Let the marbles cool in the icy water for three minutes. Discard any that have actually broken.

5. Dry the marbles with a soft towel. Then, apply a large dot of super glue or a similarly strong adhesive to the underside of a bell cap. Press firmly onto a marble, hold for a minute or so, and allow to dry for 24 hours.

6. Using the pliers and one hand, gently pry open one of the jump rings.

7. Thread the open jump ring through the center of your chain, to the end of the keychain or around the ribbon. Then, thread it through the hole atop the bell cap on the marble.

8. Your creation is complete—and striking. If you'd prefer to hang each marble from a ribbon, they make stunning prisms when displayed in a sunlit window.

Activity 2

GOOD CLEAN FUN: PETRI DISHES, GEODES AND POPSICLES

Ready, Set

Here's what you'll need:

- meltable soap blocks and coloring (from any craft store)

- popsicle sticks

- popsicle mold

- one marble

- petri dish or small, flat glass ramekin

- cooking spray

- eyedropper and toothpick.

Go!

We've proved the point. Being rigid gets you snapped, cracked or shattered. Not good. And certainly not happy. But, a little bit of change at a time, some care with the material (or person) in question and the results can be very different.

We'd been introducing Gavin to the concept of states of matter: solids, liquids and gasses. And (because the older two knew Mom's story by now), we ran through a little game altogether. First, we pretended we were happy little molecules. We were comfy. Not too hot and not too cold. We kind of sloshed around like "hippie" molecules, fluid and groovy. Hey, man. I'm a liquid. What's your gig?

Then, suddenly, somebody turned down the heat! (This is when Maura and Sean know to begin hamming it up.) Our teeth were chattering. We shivered and drew close together for warmth. Closer. Closer! It was cold, and we little molecules moved in tightly. We couldn't move much now, but we were a lot happier all densely bunched up, like one solid group (because yes, the change in temperature had caused us to become a solid).

Now, the thermostat went in the other direction! It was practically tropical! First, we moved back to sloshy happiness. But soon, it was even too hot for that. We started to push each other away. "Give me room, I'm sweltering here!" we shouted testily, each of us floating off in a different direction. Turn up the heat, and the solid became a liquid, which became a gas.

Rather than breaking like the rigid glass, we had simply "gone along" with the stress of change. We'd changed, but even in different forms, we remained true to who we were. That's being "cooked spaghetti." Whole and a whole lot more pliable.

A wonderfully fun way to experiment with changing states of matter is soap-making. Now, I know it may sound a little bohemian—maybe too challenging, even. But I promise you—if a three-year-old can manage it with craft store materials, you most certainly can, too.

The O'Toole Asperkids each chose a unique "soapy" adventure using the same underlying process. Store-bought glycerin soap and goat's milk soap both had to be cut from bricks we bought, then diced up using a simple kitchen knife. This makes the melting process faster.

We followed the step-by-step directions on the packaging to tell us how long to microwave the measuring cups containing soap chunks. In small bursts, we heated and stirred, giving Gavin a good chance to practice counting backwards with the timer and his siblings some well-supervised practice chopping the larger bricks as the first round melted.

Kapow! Just like in our "play," the heat had turned the solid into a liquid—but it was most definitely still soap (VERY hot soap—be careful!).

We squeezed in a few drops of soap color and mixed the whole concoction together. Making sure to coat the inside of our dollar-store popsicle mold with cooking spray, Gavin worked that nozzle like an only somewhat-frustrated pro, and then carefully filled the chambers with liquid soap.

Into the freezer it went to harden (thanks to the effects of cold on liquid).

Sean's soap looked fancier, but was actually even easier. He simply melted, colored and poured the glycerin soap into a Petri dish we had from a home science kit. Then, he used various combinations of toothpicks and even an eye dropper to scatter globs and streaks of extra color onto the cooled surface. It was, he decided, E Coli. An ironic—and I thought, pretty witty—choice for hand washing.

And Maura's creation? Well, that girl's always gotta have some bling. Her soap was no different. Maura made a geode. First we melted some of the goat's milk soap to the point where it was play-dough consistency. We hand-molded this bit around a single marble.

Maura colored and dyed several more rounds, mixing purples and even grays and browns, building each layer around the previous one. Finally, she rolled the uneven, lumpy "rock" in some black cake glitter (not very soapy, but the effect was great and it'd wash off, anyway!).

Then it, too, went into the freezer.

About an hour later, the popsicles came out, ready for us to insert the wooden sticks. The geode, too, was done. Mom got to do the honors of very carefully slicing the "rock" open with a chef's knife until I touched the marble, then rotating it around the center point. Maura pulled the halves apart, pried out the marble and, lo and behold, we had made geode soap!

I'm not sure which project I could possibly say was coolest. Each creation was amazing, truly representing the child who had made it.

And through every change—the heating, dying, molding, pouring, layering and cooling—we saw that the soap never cracked, never broke, never fell apart because, unlike the glass marble, it adapted. It remained cohesive. It was always soap, but it bent and moved and took the shape of the situation (or container) in which it was placed.

In the same way, I reminded them, if they use their words to explain their feelings, if they will consider multiple perspectives and rely upon smart coping strategies—they will NOT crack. They will, instead, be their own creations, *whole*, authentic and completely amazing.

Activity 3

PERMISSIBLE BREAKTHROUGHS: NINE WAYS TO PLAY WITH BUBBLE WRAP

Ready, Set
Here's what you'll need:

- bubble wrap

- index cards

- permanent markers.

Go!
Usually, when you hear the word "break," whatever follows isn't going to be good. Break up. Break down. The one exception, though, is breakthrough. Asperkids are magnificent, talented people. Sometimes, though, it can be hard to hear their ideas above the meltdown. Or to listen to their dreams when anxiety keeps them sequestered.

NTs have a common misconception that we, Aspies, don't really want friends. That we are fine being alone. But those are two very different things.

Yes, Asperkids require more alone time than other kids. That is NOT the same thing as not feeling lonely. Aspies want friends; often, though, we don't really know how to choose good ones. When you feel anxious, rejected or afraid, the want of companionship can feel bottomless. So it's easy to compromise who we are and accept far less kindness than we deserve. I know. I've been there. I've accepted bruises and excused them. I've been the popular one too, standing in the center of the crowd, yet feeling utterly alone.

How do you make a friend? In the end, it's really very simple. You decide to take a chance. You say, "Hi." You may be ignored. You may fall in love. There's no way to tell. In fact, only this *is* certain: every friendship, every love, every adventure and reunion began with a risk and a single simple word. Everything wonderful begins with, "Hello."

And every "hello" gets us one step closer to those Asperkids. Breaking through those protective walls, letting our love in and their brilliance out.

On the surface, none of these activities is about friendship or inflexible thinking. That's good. Sometimes, a direct hit to someone's defenses will make him fight or flee with greater vehemence. Be subtle. Just mention, as you go, how piercing, popping and punching through *can* be good—in fact, with the right people, at the right times, it can even be great.

Bubble Wrap Fabulosity

I love Alfred Fielding and Marc Chavannes. Odds are your Asperkid does, too. In 1957, these two engineers harnessed the beauty of the bubble, creating the now-beloved packaging hero: bubble wrap. Now, there are even online, virtual bubble wrap websites. But, I really don't think they even come close to the real poppety-pop-pop fabulousness. Other people must agree: Office Depot, for example, sells enough bubble wrap each year to wrap around the earth. Twice. There are more than 250 Facebook pages devoted to bubble wrap, and an entire tome—*The Bubble Wrap Book* (Green 1998)—was even published, full of (crazy?) ingenious possibilities for the stuff, from bicycle helmet construction to low-tech burglar alarms.

What's the allure, the big draw of these sheets of plastic blisters? "The act of popping Bubble Wrap is almost like a catharsis," one marketing executive said during the 50th anniversary celebration a few years ago. "It's a little indulgence in some small act of destruction that is neither dangerous nor offensive" (Fernandez 2004).

Pop. Pop.

Don't tell the Asperkids, but bubble wrap is also a ridiculously awesome way to give proprioceptive sensory input (which is calming) underfoot *or* in-hand, strengthen the pincer grip (which affects handwriting), coordination and visual perception. And if a child's pincer (pointer plus thumb) isn't strong enough, all you need to do is guide him to pop bubbles with his thumb, index and middle fingers (and ring finger, too, if necessary).

Variations on the Fun

Using colored permanent markers, bubble wrap can become almost any kind of fun you want—just remember to throw in the occasional remark about a hug, a hello or a smile acting like "people poppers," breaking through sad moods or scared feelings and letting in the fun. Try some of these ideas with the Asperkids in your life:

- **Travel bingo:** Make travel time more fun! On large bubbles, draw stop signs, school buses, a garbage truck, trees and anything else you'd like the Asperkids to "spy" during a car trip, time in the airport or even on a train. When they see a real stop sign or tree or truck, POP! You can offer a prize for when it's complete: a clear sheet for free popping!

- **Letter match:** Write capital letters on a stack of index cards and lots of different lower-case letters on individual bubbles; then let the Asperkid go through the cards one by one, only popping the letter matches. Use the same idea to practice print-to-cursive recognition by writing a letter in cursive on the bubble wrap and in print on the paper. Find the match and pop!

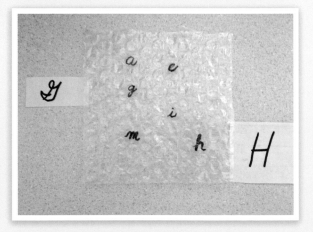

- **Geometry pop:** Write out the name of a shape (like quadrilateral or hexagon) and on the bubble wrap, write number choices. The Asperkid has to correctly identify the number of sides or corners for the shape in question. Beginners can look at outlines to help remember or count; challenge more advanced learners to draw out their own models, if they're needed.

- **Quantity comprehension:** Show a number and ask the Asperkid to pop that many bubbles, practicing their understanding of one-to-one correspondence.

- **Word to number:** Display the written word "two" or "seven" (etc.) and mark the bubble wrap with numerals. The goal is to match the number to the word (i.e. "six" and "6").

- **Color search:** Using different markers, color in the bubbles so that they look like confetti. Show the Asperkid color words (you can even begin by writing "pink" in pink letters, and so on, as a clue for emerging readers), and ask her to pop the color you've named.

- **Multiplication set-up:** Color in multiple groups of the same quantity of bubbles (numerous pairs of two darkened bubbles, for example). Then, show a card which says "Three groups of two (3 × 2)." The Asperkid can pop each set of the multiplicand, skip counting or count one by one to get to the product. "Two (pop, pop), four (pop, pop), six (pop, pop). Three groups of two is six." You can also practice basic skip counting by writing the multiples of any number which the Asperkid then pops in order (throw in decoy answers when he's ready!): 4, 8, 12, 16 and so on…

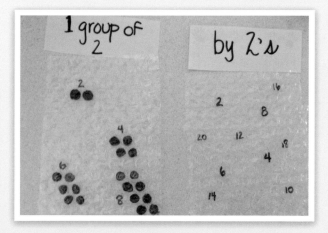

More "breakthrough fun" on the next page, too!

Activity 4

POMANDERS, TATTOOED BANANAS AND CONSTELLATIONS

Ready, Set
Here's what you'll need:

- orange

- whole cloves

- one tablespoon each: ground cinnamon, nutmeg, cloves

- sandalwood oil (from natural food stores)

- paper bag

- bananas

- pencil with eraser

- needle or straight pin

- print out of a cartoon or line drawing

- paper plate, cardboard or laminated special interest photo

- yarn

- plastic knitting needle

- hole punch

- silver thread

- regular sewing needle

- black Styrofoam tray from butcher department

- rubber band

- masking tape

- colorful foam board

- colorful cardboard.

Go!

One of my favorite Montessori tools is called a pin-punch or pin-poke. It's basically a wooden handle attached to a needle-like metal shaft. With a little bit of diligence (and undetected fine motor work and practiced hand-eye coordination), kids can use it to poke tiny holes right next to one another, and actually "cut out" any shape they'd like—be it a square, a buffalo or North America (we have all three on display at the moment). You can approximate the same tool by pushing a straight pin or needle into the eraser end of a short pencil. The pencil itself becomes the handle your child will grasp while poking with the pin or needle (be sure to place a felt pad, cutting board or cork board beneath the project to protect your table).

What can you do with pin pokes besides popping outlined creatures out of paper? Awesome stuff, that's what. For example:

Pomander

An orange becomes a beautiful sensory experience (and holiday keepsake) with just a rubber band or masking tape, your pin-poke and cloves. Since medieval times, pomanders have been favorite natural air fresheners (nobility would even hold them close so as not to breathe in the stench of the common folk), not to mention that they make a lovely way to add some citrus perfume to any season. Here's all you do:

1. Wrap the orange with rings of rubber bands or masking tape (help guide the Asperkid to learn to hold the fruit while also stretching open the bands).

2. Using the bands or tape as a guide to make straight lines, pierce holes all around the fruit, trying to evenly space as many as possible.

3. Into each hole, the Asperkids should insert a whole clove, pressing in as deeply as possible.

4. Put the finished pomander into a paper bag with the cinnamon, nutmeg, ground cloves and sandalwood oil (these act as a natural preservative). Shake to coat. (Ideally, you should leave them in the bag for three weeks, shaking it up every few days—that's if you want the pomanders to keep for several years!)

5. Place the pomanders in a cool, dry, shady place, tying each with pretty ribbon for gift-giving or stacking them in a pyramid for display. The Asperkids (and any other kids!) will be delighted with the fantastically fragrant results.

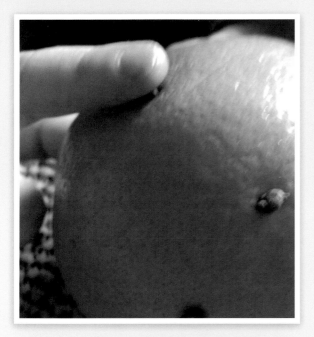

Tattooed Bananas (Quite Possibly One of My All-Time Favorite Things EVER)

We all know that a banana left to the open air will oxidize, turning the flesh brown. Well, you may not have realized that the peel will do the same—rapidly. A little strategic know-how, and this lunchbox staple becomes the ultimate kid canvas.

1. Print out or sketch the outline of anything your Asperkid loves (mine chose a beloved Muppets character, Iron Man and George Washington, the first American president). Tape it to the banana peel, cutting small slits into the paper to help it lie as flat as possible.

2. Firmly but gently (you don't want to squish the fruit out!), hold the banana steady while you move along the outline, "tattooing" little pin prick holes through the paper and peel wherever there are marks in the picture. What you are actually doing is artfully breaking through the cell walls in the banana peel and allowing oxygen to rush in, causing a chemical change (oxidation) to occur wherever you make holes.

3. Leave the banana for 5 to 10 minutes and then remove the paper. I promise, one tattooed banana, and you will never eat a plain one again (this is also a fun way to write "secret" messages to leave on the breakfast table).

Lacing Plates and Star Sewing

1. Lacing cards are a classic activity because of the multitude of skills they engage…plus they're really fun. That's especially true if they *mean* something to the kiddo using them.

2. To make a younger child's personalized lacing card, use a basic hole punch to create a freestyle design in a paper plate that features a favorite character (we have a *lot* of Spiderman lacing cards around our house).

3. Alternatively, you can use colorful foam board or cardboard and the hole punch to "write" the child's name or make shapes.

4. For an older Asperkid, print out a family picture or special interest photo (the Tardis, a dinosaur, a map) onto cardstock and laminate it for durability. Then, outline the portrait with punched holes.

5. Show the Asperkid how to tie a fat knot in one end of a piece of yarn and thread the other end through a plastic needle. Pull it once through the first hole in the card, demonstrate the up, through, pull/down, through, pull pattern and what to do if a hole is skipped or a mistake happens (great practice for the "So what? I can fix this" mentality!).

6. If you happen to have one of the black Styrofoam trays often used under meat or fresh fruit by the grocer, give it a good wash with soap and hot water. Then, give it to an older Asperkid as the perfect card for "Star Sewing." Just lay a paper print out of a constellation on the black tray, and have your Asperkid pin-poke or needle-poke where the stars are. Take away the paper, thread the needle with silver thread (teaching your kiddo how to get it through the needle's eye and tie the knot), and poke through an "endpoint" star from the back side. Sew down, through, and up again at each star in the constellation—and even add some spray silver glitter if you really want to jazz it up. When she's done, your Asperkid will have a scientifically accurate, artistically rendered upcycled star map! Pierce. Poke. Punch. Have fun breaking through and letting the wonder in.

Snapshot-Sized Fun

SLIME. 'NUFF SAID

Ready, Set

What lies in-between solid and liquid? Slime. It's runny. It's goopey. It's gross…and it's Mad Science awesome.

Here's all you'll need:

- two teaspoons of Borax powder

- two cups of white school glue

- food coloring

- Bowl A: 1⅓ cups warm water in one bowl

- Bowl B: 1½ cups warm water in another bowl

- OR the same quantities of glowing water (see our recipe on page 124).

Go!

1. Mix the Borax into Bowl A thoroughly.

2. Blend the glue into Bowl B.

3. Slowly combine the bowls (adding the food coloring), blending well…and you've got slime!

4. If you want a thicker "Flubber" feel, use three teaspoons of Borax instead.

Pour it through your fingers, holes in plastic baskets (suspend them for a shower effect), squish it, bounce it, smash it or pull it into a rope shape. Being "flexible" makes almost anything possible!

CONCLUSION

Everything that is right and natural about learning and wonder and curiosity and peace is already inside our children. All of them. It's just up to us to make sure they feel safe enough and invested enough to let their natural aptitudes take over.

Spectrum kids may not progress through development as smoothly or predictably as typical children, or they may sail through one aspect and get stuck on another. A sort of growing-up jet lag. But our children most certainly do require the same sense of physical peace and self-sufficiency in order to build psychological calm and confidence.

Above all, Asperkids—like all kids— want the joy of learning that they are capable, important, relevant human beings. Yes, there are countless practical, academic, physical, social and emotional skills that we MUST demonstrate, explain and repeat. But they deserve to learn those lessons while having FUN.

Whether you are an educator, a parent or a clinician, teach as you would want to learn. Make it interesting. Make it fun. Our success, and our kids' success, depend on how well we respect their individual dignity and empower their natural gifts.

Play, it's been said, is the brain's favorite way of learning. While play looks different for different people, wonder, kindness and joy are universal. So, we have carefully woven wit, humor and discovery into this *Asperkid's Game Plan*. We've made room for both facts *and* feelings. For trial *and* triumph. For everything and for everyone. Within our fun, there is—and will always be—a never-ending celebration of the possible and of the amazing kids who will dream it into being.

TRIANGLE CHALLENGES

Try These Star Challenges!

- Construct a four-pointed star with four triangles.

- Construct a six-pointed star with six triangles.

- Construct a 12-pointed star with 12 triangles.

- Use six triangles for a hexagon (with a hexagonal opening in the center).

- Use 12 triangles to form an open 12-pointed star with a dodecagon (12-sided polygon) in the center. Remove one star at a time—the dodecagon will become other polygons—see if you can name them!

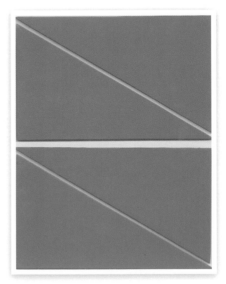

Tangram Puzzlers

Tangrams are seven-piece puzzles that originated in ancient China. By rearranging the pieces into different formations, players can create an almost endless stream of shapes and pictures—as well as deepening understanding of geometry, problem-solving and critical thinking skills. Plus, they are really fun! Try these challenges, then see what your Asperkids can create on their own.

- Use two (then three, four, five and six) pieces to form a triangle.

- Use seven pieces to make a trapezoid, then a rhombus.

- How many ways can you build a square? A rectangle?

- Copy these pictures and build a house, then a boat.

- Printable tangram puzzles are available from the Museum of Play at www.museumofplay.org/flash-games/tangrams/tangram_grid.pdf and endless other websites. Just google "tangram" and see where it leads you!

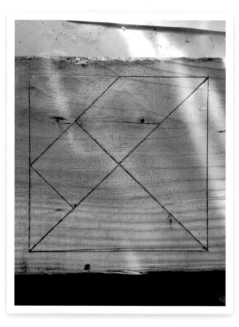

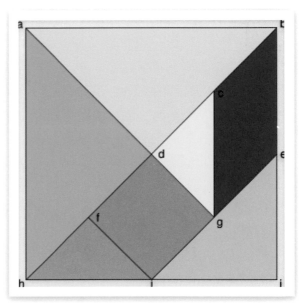

CAST-A-NET PAPER SHAPE TEMPLATES

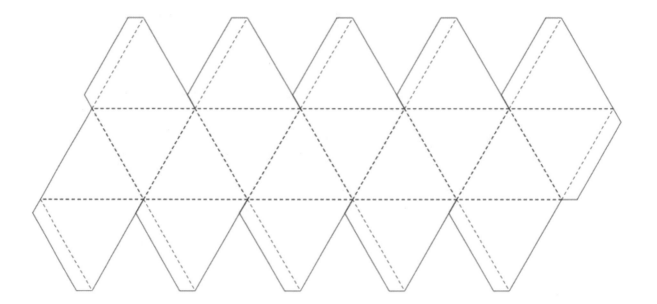

TEMPLATE I

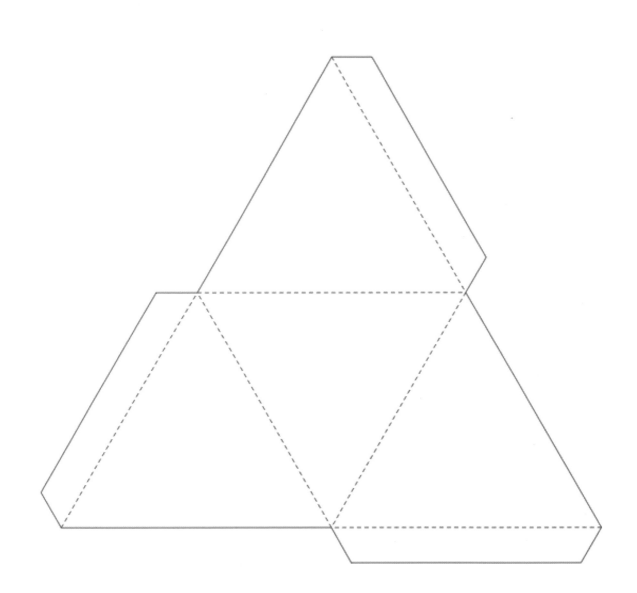

TEMPLATE 2

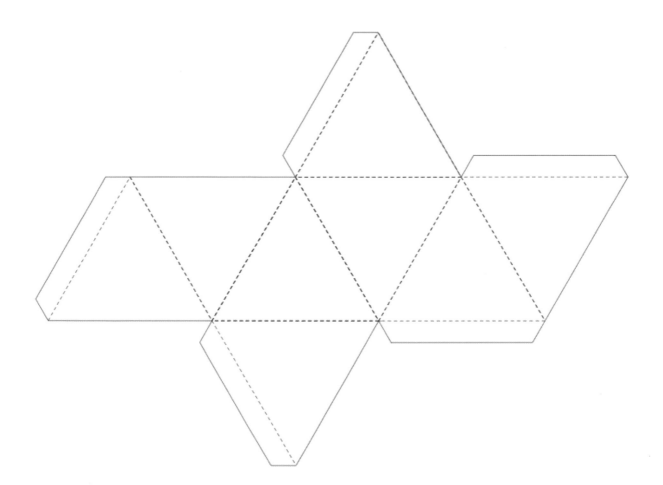

TEMPLATE 3

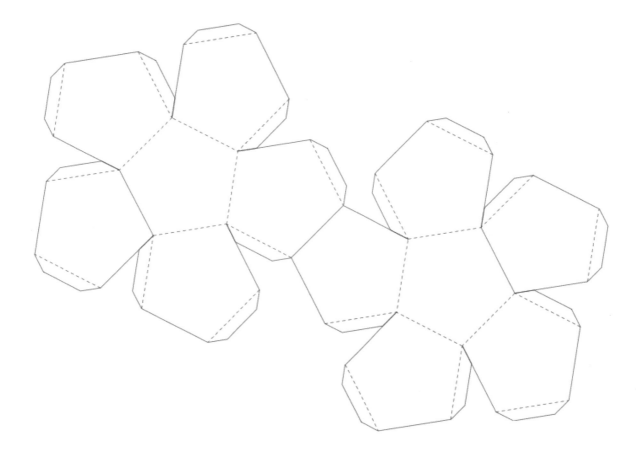

TEMPLATE 4

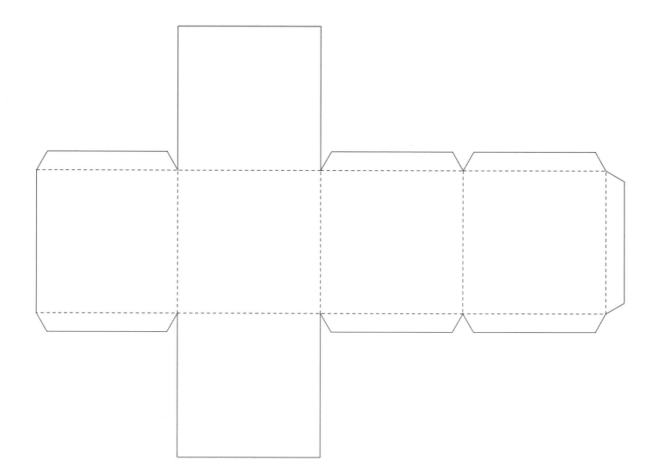

TEMPLATE 5

RESOURCES FOR MORE FUN (AND UNDERCOVER DISCOVERIES)

Online
Asperkids Blog
Recognized by Disney's Babble.com as being among the world's top autism blogs in three categories: Parents of Young Children, For Teens and By a Young Person.

My words, frequently updated with creative ideas and a healthy dose of humor.
www.asperkids.com/asperkids-blog

AK Shop-for-the-Kids
A sweet suite of curated collections that benefits Asperkids everywhere. Featuring the Asperkids Sensory Line, collaborations with ThinkFun Games (like Rush Hour and Tip Over), Montessori Services tools for learning and scores of creative, independent artisans. Proceeds support kids on the spectrum!
www.asperkids.com/akshop

"Purposeful Play" Favorites
From Asperkids and ThinkFun

- The Asperkids Collection—ALL GAMES

From Asperkids and Montessori Services

- Mighty Mind and Super Mind

- Fractiles

- Wooden tangram (ancient Chinese puzzle)

- Book of paper airplanes and origami paper

- Unplugged Play

- Rainbow beeswax honeycomb candle kit

- Sunprint kit

- National Gallery of Art Up Close Card Game

- Can you find it? I Spy at the Metropolitan Museum of Art

- Shut the Box game

- Pattern play

- Set Card game

- Quirkle

- 50 optical illusions cards

- Language objects—all, or in boxed collections

- Mystery bag and blindfold set

- Electricity and magnetic combination kit (circuit kit featured in "Asperkids")

Asperkids on Pinterest
Thousands of photo links to unimaginable quantities of FUN.
www.pinterest.com/Asperkids

Paper Models of Polyhedra
Polyhedra are beautiful 3-D geometrical figures that have fascinated philosophers, mathematicians and artists for millennia. On this site are a few hundred paper models available for free. Just click on a picture to go to a page with a net of the model.
www.korthalsaltes.com

Pathways for Learning
Handwriting and written expression tools designed by the same occupational therapy expert who bullet-pointed the skills developed in this book.
www.shop.pathwaysforlearning.com

The Pointillator!
Have some dotty fun making your own pointillism online with the Pointillator!
www.incredibleart.org/links/pointillator.html

Supercoloring—Paint the World
Hundreds of free, printable PDFs for coloring or using as references for making your mural.
www.supercoloring.com

ViHart—Recreational Mathematics

This chick ROCKS. She will, I promise, make even the most ardent math-o-phobe say, "That. Is. SOOOOO cool!" Math doodling, balloon twisting, music box experiments, food and even links to her online Khan Academy classes, including Sick Number Games and Fruit by the Foot.

www.vihart.com/everything

REFERENCES

Cook O'Toole, J. (2012) *The Asperkid's (Secret) Book of Social Rules: The Handbook of Not-So-Obvious Social Guidelines for Tweens and Teens with Asperger Syndrome*. London: Jessica Kingsley Publishers.

Cook O'Toole, J. (2013) *The Asperkid's Launch Pad: Home Design to Empower Everyday Superheroes*. London: Jessica Kingsley Publishers.

Fernandez, D. (2004) "Bubble wrap: A pop culture sensation that packs endless pleasure." *Seattle Pi Online*. Available at www.seattlepi.com/lifestyle/article/Bubble-Wrap-A-pop-culture-sensation-that-packs-1162675.php, accessed on 26 November 2013.

Green, J. (1998) *The Bubble Wrap Book*. New York: Harper Perennial.